In *Letting Go of the Need to Be R*
winsome storytelling, recounts
braced through acquiring vario
never be good enough distorted .... would become a frenzied performance-based life. Welcome home, Jeff! I highly recommend his deeply revealing book to those who desperately need to discover God's love, acceptance, and forgiveness so they can find rest and peace from their tortured search for significance.

—John Arnott, Toronto, Catch the Fire and Partners In Harvest

Letting Go of the Need to Be Right is a great book on humility, hunger, and honor by Jeff Dollar, a man who has been a friend for the last fifteen years. You teach what you know, but you reproduce who you are. I am a firm believer you cannot take others where you have not been yourself. *Letting Go of the Need to Be Right* takes you on a journey to discover the truth about lies that hold you captive. Imagine what your life would look like if you were totally free. An ocean of grace is waiting for the humble.

—Leif Hetland, president, Global Mission Awareness,
and author of *Call to Reign* and *Giant Slayers!*

Jeff hits the bull's eye in his book *Letting Go of the Need to Be Right*. It's gripping, reaching, and life changing. You will be glad you read this.

—R T Kendall, minister of Westminster Chapel (1977–2002),
author, and speaker

I loved reading Jeff Dollar's engaging book, *Letting Go of the Need to Be Right*. I promise you, it will be easy to identify with Jeff's journey, and you'll love the insights he gives you on authentic humility. This is a great read for couples, leaders … just about everybody! Oh, don't skip over chapter 9, "Letting Others Win." This book can change your life!

—Brian Simmons, Passion & Fire Ministries
and The Passion Translation Project

I guarantee you will see areas of your life that need the transforming power of the Holy Spirit by reading Jeff's book *Letting Go of the Need to Be Right*. I know because I just finished reading it.

—Don Finto, pastor emeritus of Belmont Church
and founder of the Caleb Company

Jeff Dollar is a master at letting go of the need to be right! Having worked with him for over ten years, we know him to be one of the meekest people we've ever met. What he writes in this book is not theory but workplace-tested truth. We encourage you to read this book and apply its principles. The people you lead will thank you!

—Alyn and A. J. Jones, senior associate pastors, Grace Centers

FOREWORD BY Danny Silk

LETTING GO
OF THE NEED TO BE
RIGHT

Experience the Power of Humility

JEFF DOLLAR

BroadStreet
PUBLISHING

BroadStreet Publishing® Group, LLC
Savage, Minnesota, USA
BroadStreetPublishing.com

Letting Go of the Need to Be Right: EXPERIENCE THE POWER OF HUMILITY

Copyright © 2019 by Jeff Dollar

978-1-4245-4990-0 (softcover)
978-1-4245-5061-6 (e-book)

All rights reserved. No part of this book may be reproduced in any form, except for brief quotations in printed reviews, without permission in writing from the publisher.

Unless otherwise indicated, Scripture quotations are taken from the Holy Bible, New Living Translation, copyright © 1996, 2004, 2007 by Tyndale House Foundation. Used by permission of Tyndale House Publishers, Inc., Carol Stream, Illinois 60188, USA. All rights reserved. Scripture quotations marked TPT are from The Passion Translation®. Copyright © 2017, 2018 by BroadStreet Publishing Group, ThePassionTranslation.com. Used by permission. Scripture quotations marked NKJV are taken from the New King James Version. Copyright © 1982 by Thomas Nelson, Inc. Used by permission. All rights reserved. Scripture quotations marked NIV are taken from the Holy Bible, New International Version®, NIV® Copyright ©1973, 1978, 1984, 2011 by Biblica, Inc.® Used by permission. All rights reserved worldwide. Scripture quotations marked ESV are taken from The Holy Bible, English Standard Version. Copyright © 2000; 2001 by Crossway Bibles, a division of Good News Publishers. Used by permission. All rights reserved. Scripture quotations marked NASB are taken from the New American Standard Bible, © Copyright 1960, 1962, 1963, 1968, 1971, 1972, 1973, 1975, 1977, 1995 by The Lockman Foundation. Used by permission. Scripture quotations marked AMP are taken from the Amplified® Bible, copyright © 2015 by The Lockman Foundation. Used by permission. Scripture quotations marked AMPC are taken from the Amplified® Bible (AMPC), Copyright © 1954, 1958, 1962, 1964, 1965, 1987 by The Lockman Foundation Used by permission. www.Lockman.org. Scripture quotations marked NIrV are taken from the Holy Bible, New International Reader's Version®, NIrV® Copyright © 2014 ,1998 ,1996 ,1995 by Biblica, Inc.™ Used by permission of Zondervan. All rights reserved worldwide. www.zondervan.com The "NIrV" and "New International Reader's Version" are trademarks registered in the United States Patent and Trademark Office by Biblica, Inc.™ Scripture quotations marked TLB are taken from the THE LIVING BIBLE (TLB): Scripture taken from THE LIVING BIBLE copyright© 1971. Used by permission of Tyndale House Publishers, Inc., Carol Stream, Illinois 60188. All rights reserved.

All italics in Scripture quotations are those of the author and meant to indicate emphasis.

Stock or custom editions of BroadStreet Publishing titles may be purchased in bulk for educational, business, ministry, fundraising, or sales promotional use. For information, please email info@broadstreetpublishing.com.

Cover and interior by Garborg Design at garborgdesign.com

Printed in the United States of America
19 20 21 22 23 5 4 3 2 1

Contents

To my wife, Becky, and my children, Bethany and Joel.

Becky, thank you for your patience. I have learned and continue to learn so much from you. You have taught me that the first one to say "I'm sorry" actually wins. You are the kindest person I know. I love you with all my heart.

To Bethany and Joel, you both continue to amaze me. I am so grateful for your tender and forgiving hearts. I am so proud of you both. I love you.

Acknowledgments

This book could not have been written without the help of some very special people:

To my darling wife, Becky. Thank you for the patience you have always shown me. Especially in the years I was *learning* to let go of the need to be right! To my wonderful children, Bethany and Joel, thank you for your patience and encouragement while I practiced all that's in this book. You three—more than anyone else—have seen the ugly learning process behind trying to die to self. Thank you for the love, laughter, and support along the way.

Writing a book is a painstaking endeavor that is never a solo activity. Deb, without your help, there would be no book. Literally. To Jessica and Bethany, your hard work in helping me write and rewrite helped more than you know. And many thanks to the BroadStreet Publishing team for their editing, typesetting, and design work.

To my former pastors: Mark and Bev, Dave and Peggy, and Brian and Susan, thank you for making a way for me where there was no way. You recognized something in me, even though I was reluctant to believe it myself, and you consistently encouraged me through my growing pains. I sincerely thank each one of you for this investment. I would not be where I am today without each one of you pouring into my life. Thank you.

Finally, to the incredible staff at Grace Center—thank you for everything you do to make this church such a wonderful place for hosting the presence of God. Thank you for continued encouragement and support. You are a treasure and a gift to me.

Foreword

By Danny Silk

So much about leadership is confidence and discernment. It's about knowing why you are doing something and knowing when to do it. Did you do the right thing? Was it the right timing? Did you move too quickly? Did you delay too long? It's often such a risky role. The leadership role requires high levels of confidence and certainty. We practice this intentional, determined posture day in and day out. Nothing less will serve our people well. No one wants an insecure, hesitant, indecisive leader.

Confidence is believing that God can and will accomplish what He has called us to do in life. The result of all this confident leadership practice is momentum. As a result, we build a strong confidence in our own voice. We have an internal rigidity that develops. We start to trust our own voice so much that we begin to bolster our own opinions and desires as more valuable than any others. And, because we have such confidence in our decision consistency, we naturally create a culture of trusting our personal strength: "This company (family, organization, church) is successful because of my rightness." To challenge the leaders in their rightness is to challenge success and to be disloyal to the strongest part of the organization: the leadership.

As I mentioned before, no one wins with an insecure, hesitant leader, but equally awful is the leader who is impervious to input or feedback. The exact counterbalance to great confidence in a leader is equal amounts of humility. By humility, I mean the attention to learn how other people experience us. We make it a priority to gain this information. Strong, mature leaders welcome input from those around them. They've slayed the inner dragons that rise up at opposing views, they've learned to honor perspectives they have not yet seen, and they can include information in their decisions that did not originate within them. These leaders are learning, growing, and gaining new information every day—on purpose. We really do not have accurate information about what is going on inside other people until we welcome it, until we ask. Today, maybe more than ever, this a key leadership quality and skill.

We benefit because we now know how to make key adjustments in relationships, conversations, or decisions. Our rightness is more accurate than ever because our information is cleaner and more accurate than ever. Being right doesn't have to be sacrificed, but having to be the one who is right needs to go.

Jeff Dollar has written a book that I think will help us all on this journey. His speaking from personal experience and showing us what and how to change is both humorous and inspirational. Jeff is a successful leader who is about to invite you into a personal journey of how to grow from the inside out. I'm happy to introduce to you *Letting Go of the Need to Be Right*, and I highly recommend this book to you. Get out your pen and paper, highlighter, favorite beverage, and something to wipe your eyes with, because this is going to a hilarious adventure!

Danny Silk
President of Loving on Purpose Life Academy
Author of *Keep Your Love On, Powerful and Free*,
and *Business of Honor*

Introduction

When asked why the subject of "letting go of the need to be right" was important enough to be the subject of my first book, I answered, "Because it was a revelatory moment in my life when God shifted my perspective and my paradigm and I found a freedom that I had never known before."

It opened up a new world for me. Before, I couldn't hear what people were saying to me because, unknowingly, I had a driving distrust of the messengers that God put in my life because I was looking through the lens of a young man who never measured up. Therefore, it was simple and logical: If people couldn't see how hard I was trying, if they couldn't see how much I wanted to please everybody, and if they couldn't see how badly I wanted to rise up to every expectation and do everything perfectly, why would I trust them to speak into my life? My life had become one of performance. Worth had to be earned. Everybody knew that, right?

When a person, young or old, feels they have no voice, they will ultimately feel they have no worth. That was the internal drive spinning in the back of my heart. And I was completely unaware of it.

So what's the point of all these stories that I'm about to share? And what does any of it have to do with the need to be right? Well, I discovered that it was the development of this infrastructure of beliefs that were not in alignment with how God feels about me and who He says I am in His Word, that caused within me a desperate need to be right.

I heard Bill Johnson say this: "I cannot afford to have a thought in my head about me that God doesn't have in His about me." I did not know that I equated being right with being worthy. I had no idea that my thoughts were so far from His truth. Having said that, what I am trying to do here is to share my journey into that pit of spiritual blindness and show how it happened with such normalcy that I am hoping that maybe, in some way, you can relate.

My friends Betsy and Chester Kylstra, founders of Restoring the Foundations ministry, give an incredible definition and teaching on a harmful belief system that a person develops apart from God's truth. They call them "ungodly beliefs," and here the Kylstras briefly describe how they can be formed in a person's life: "Everyone, to some extent, lives out of wrong beliefs. Ungodly beliefs are 'lies' about ourselves, about others, and about God. They are dangerous because they affect all of our perceptions, all of our decisions, and all of our actions. It is easy to see why God wants our minds renewed."[1]

> Don't copy the behavior and customs of
> this world, but let God transform you into
> a new person by changing the way you
> think. Then you will know what God wants
> you to do, and you will know how good
> and pleasing and perfect His will really is.
> (Romans 12:2)

What is a belief system? It includes our beliefs, decisions,

---

1. Restoring The Foundations, *Healing and Freedom* (Hendersonville, NC: Restoring the Foundations, 2016), 35.

attitudes, agreements, judgments, expectations, vows, and oaths. Any beliefs that agree with God (His Word, His nature, His character, etc.) are our godly beliefs. Any beliefs that do not agree with God (His Word, His nature, His character, etc.) are ungodly beliefs. Our beliefs affect who we are; how we perceive ourselves; and how we relate to others, to the world around us, and to God. They determine how Christlike we become, and they even determine the quality of our Christian lives. The ungodly beliefs can be like a vise grip, putting tight constraints on our lives, choking out the abundant life that Jesus promised.

- An ungodly belief is a belief or attitude that does not agree with the Word of God, His character, or His nature.
- Beliefs are formed from the facts of our experiences.
- We sometimes inherit wrong beliefs from our families or receive them from our friends or our culture.
- Ungodly beliefs are lies that have been formed in us, often in childhood, about ourselves, about others, and about God. They are formed out of our experiences.

The "perfect" ungodly belief is one that appears to be absolutely *true* based on the *facts* of our experience and yet is absolutely *false*. Even though these beliefs are completely false, most people who think this way do not even realize it. Until an ungodly belief is pointed out to us, we continue on, day after day, living our life based on a lie.

I have reflected on how scarily unaware I was of the lies that developed the filtration system of self-defense and protection that were woven into my life through the development of this subtle yet incredibly powerful belief system that cultivated throughout my journey of failures and successes. The most important part of this, though, was how far I was from being able to walk in the intimacy and power of humility that held the key to the freedom that I didn't know I needed. So, at the end of each relevant chapter in this book, I have made a list of the ungodly beliefs that developed during that particular part of my life.

Fortunately, God in His kindness and mercy intervened and drew me into a place of tender revelation that was pivotal to my life and destiny. He revealed to me that I was bound up in self-protection, that my self-worth was tied to my need to be right, and that few people lived up to my expectation of what a messenger from God would look like. So thank you for your willingness to walk with me as I once again ponder the pathways in and out of that dark pit of isolation and bondage.

> Bless the Lord, O my soul, and all that is
> within me, bless his holy name … who
> redeems your life from the pit, who
> crowns you with steadfast love and mercy.
> (Psalm 103:1, 4 ESV)

The Way of a Fool

As snow in summer and rain in harvest,
so honor is not fitting for a fool.
Like a flitting sparrow, like a flying swallow,
so a curse without cause shall not alight.
A whip for the horse, and a bridle for a donkey,
and a rod for the fool's back.
Do not answer a fool according to his folly,
lest you also be like him.
Answer a fool according to his folly,
lest he be wise in his own eyes.
He who sends a message by the hand of a fool
cuts off his own feet and drinks violence.
Like the legs of the lame that hang limp
is a proverb in the mouth of fools.
Like one who binds a stone in a sling
is he who gives honor to a fool.
Like a thorn that goes into the hand of a
drunkard is a proverb in the mouth of fools.
The great God who formed everything gives
the fool his hire and the transgressor his wages.
As a dog returns to his own vomit,
so a fool repeats his folly.
Do you see a man wise in his own eyes?
There is more hope for a fool than for him.
(Proverbs 26 NKJV)

The Beginning of False Knowledge

Do you remember the first solo drive you took right after you got your driver's license? I can't guess whether most people do or don't, but I remember mine. I went directly from the thrill of victory straight to my first job interview. It was with UPS—an opportunity that my father had arranged. I had no idea at the time that my father had been a rock star with UPS. I knew he had worked there, and I knew he had a bit of influence (enough to put in a good word for his son), but I totally underestimated his stellar performance and reputation.

Sitting in the prospective employee line, I looked around and all my insecurities kept mounting—and mounting. There I was, a smashing six foot two, 130-pound stick of flesh and bones, slouched over and wishing I could bolt. To be totally transparent, I even lied on my application. I created a five-pound lie and I told them I weighed 135 pounds—like that was going to make a huge difference in my appearance and somehow make me more appealing as a potential employee.

Eventually, a gruff man stuck his head out of a room and said, "Which one of these guys is Dollar?" When I stood, I could see his tangible disappointment. You see, his productivity was directly affected by the physical abilities of his crew. He had just inherited a kid who looked like he'd had a bout with rickets.

You didn't need to have the gift of discernment to see that my new supervisor was sorely disappointed in his new employee. In my opinion, he was by nature rough, harsh, and insensitive. Whether by nature or nurture, this man was my worst nightmare. After my interview was over, one of the first things he said to me was, "Well, I don't think you're gonna make it. You just don't have what it takes to work here." He sized me up, and I simply didn't measure up to whatever his expectations were. And all that before I even began.

UPS is an amazing organization. They have to be to meet the expectations of their clientele. Their employees have to memorize zip codes, get thousands of packages delivered in a timely manner, know precisely how to pick up a box, and know how to handle spills, broken boxes, and jammed conveyor belts—just to highlight a few of the responsibilities. And all this has to be done in sweltering heat and freezing cold in an environment of intense pressure.

My first position (yes, I was hired—but only because of the respect my father had gained during his employment there) was as an "unjammer." I was in a corner, alone, and responsible for … yes, you guessed it, unjamming boxes on the conveyors. When the boxes jammed, all progress was stopped, and it was my responsibility to get things moving again.

That first night on the job was a nightmare. My job was to unjam any boxes that got caught in the conveyor belt junction, and until I could remedy the problem, everything stopped. The pressure of that was overwhelming. Intent to please, I plunged ahead. My eagerness didn't match my physical capabilities, but my tenacity won. However, my body let me know it did not appreciate this abrupt initiation. My muscles cramped like crazy and I threw up. It was not a stellar first impression.

Nonetheless, the guys at my new workplace began to appreciate my efforts, and yes, there may have been a bit of pure pity involved, but I became like their little brother. And if you're envisioning the type of big brothers like Wally was to Beaver, you have it wrong. Nope, this was the type that few sitcoms are written about—mainly because you can't air some of the things that they called me. All that said, I learned to laugh with them and roll with their antics. Actually, I didn't think I had too many choices if I wanted to continue working there. Few places paid as well as UPS, especially for part-time employees, and that provided an opportunity to for me to work while attending high school. They constantly made me aware of the fact that there were always at least seventeen people ready to take my job.

I began to feel comfortable in the corner because I was away from most people, mainly my supervisor. He had no problem publicly annihilating me. Any time I tried to advance from an "unjammer," my performance wasn't good enough, so back to the corner I went.

My supervisor's rough, harsh manner met my intimidation with a fury, and he won every time. I just buckled and internalized my humiliation. What else was I to do? Whether he was right or wrong in his criticisms really made no difference to me. All I heard were his shouts in front of my new "brothers" that I didn't measure up and couldn't do anything right. At the start of my shifts, he would often say, "Good luck, Dollar." But his tone implied the conclusion, "and you're gonna need it." I suspect he was trying to put some fight in me and that he wanted me to prove him wrong, but as hard as I worked to do it, I couldn't. I was simply filled with a paralyzing fear and doubted myself the whole time.

The physical and mental stress was always a factor in this workplace and, thankfully, not just for me. I watched as many guys just gave up. Even college athletes puked like I did on their first night in the hub. Aside from all the intensity, did I mention that it was always thirty degrees hotter inside the trucks than outside?

All that said, I was eventually promoted out of the corner, and I started to feel a bit more comfortable in my job. My body became used to the work, which was incredibly grueling. I became a "sorter." I was to sort boxes weighing up to fifty pounds that were being unloaded from a truck, and get them to the right destination. The goal was to unload as many boxes as humanly possible, because management set quotas for each employee to help the area supervisor make sure each of his employees met their hourly goals. Simply put, each employee had to keep up the pace or be fired.

* * * * *

At this point in my life, I began to believe things about myself that were not true—things that God did not say or believe about me. I had no idea that I began to invent my own stories around the events, attitudes, and actions of those around me. I would allow my imagination to figure out the reasons why people would react or respond a certain way to me. So in the middle of these experiences, I found myself believing …

- I am a failure.
- I will never measure up.
- I have no voice.
- I have no worth.
- No matter how hard I try, I will never be able to succeed.

Have you found yourself believing similar lies? Can you identity them? If so, I would encourage you to make a list and pray along with me the prayers that you will find at the end of each chapter.

Father, please reveal to me any place in my life where I am believing a lie about myself. Please give me the courage to look honestly at my heart and take responsibility for any place I have chosen to embrace deception over your truth about me. As I confess these lies to you, I ask that you help me replace them with your truth. In the name of Jesus, amen.

A Metamorphosis

Fortunately, UPS has a policy of rotating supervisors, so after a few months, it was time for a rotation to take place, and my first supervisor—let's call him "One"—rotated out and my nightmare soon turned into more of a dream, if you could call it that. My second supervisor—let's call him "Two"—was the polar opposite of my first. Astonishingly, he was even-tempered and taught by example. He had no problem getting in it with you and demonstrating how to accomplish the job more effectively. He never belittled and was always encouraging. And something monumental happened: he saw potential in me—which, frankly, was a shock.

Two's attitude was life changing for me. Trucks would roll in, and the faster the guys unloaded, the faster I had to sort. Sorters had to memorize all the zip codes in the United States and get the packages onto the correct belt. In the past, when I would get it wrong and a box with an Idaho address would be on its way to Florida, One would shout out from the catwalk above,

"Hey, Dollar, don't you know where Sioux Falls, Idaho, goes?" I felt so stupid. But throughout my shifts with Two, he would often say, "Jeff, you're doing a great job. Keep it up! You're getting better at this every day!"

The more I heard that, the more I actually believed I could do it. And an interesting thing happened. The more I believed I could do it, the more and more success I had in doing it. The more confidence he had in me, the more I had in myself. The more confidence I had in myself, the more energy and accuracy I had. The less focused I was on being afraid I was going to fail, the more quickly and precisely I mentally processed the addresses.

I was fortunate that the next supervisor after Two—let's call him "Three"—was another man who possessed wisdom and kindness similar to Two's. He would go out of his way to praise. He would find things that the workers were doing right and praise them publicly for them. To the degree that One was harsh, impatient, and belittling, Three was the complete opposite. And it wasn't just with me. He would find ways to help and encourage everyone. He would jump down off the observation platform to actually show me how to handle certain types of boxes. "Here, let me show you how to grab this size box," Three would say. "Pick it up at each corner, and if you need to, flip it like this. That way, you'll only need to have your hands on it half as long."

The more I learned from these tips, the more I valued the training. I learned that hustling would only get you so far and that working smarter was much more productive than working in a fear-inspired frenzy. This drove me to find other ways to be more efficient. I wanted to do a good job, but not just for me this time— for my supervisor as well. I wanted to make him look as good as he made me feel.

By the time Four became my supervisor, I had found my own style with this job. I knew the task at hand, and I would find ways to make it happen. Four was another amazing guy but a bit different. He looked like a rock star, rode a motorcycle, was extremely popular and likable, and became my friend. By this time, I was rapidly excelling in this workplace. I felt like a UPS superstar. I had learned how to perform well.

Too soon for me, another rotation took place, and One rolled back into the supervisor position for my team. Cringing, I also realized that I, for some unknown reason, had never had an annual employee review. Great. Just great. All these years of amazing supervisors, ones that were genuinely interested in my success, and not one of them ever wrote a yearly review of my progress. Now I found myself back under the watchful oppression of my first supervisor and he was writing my review. How ironic.

Several years had passed, several pounds had been gained, and a great deal of confidence had been acquired by me since I first walked into this man's office. Yet I was still trembling inside as I sat down before him, bracing myself for emotional impact. But this time I'd promised myself I would not let him get to me. No matter what I was feeling on the inside, I determined he would never again see me sweat under his criticisms.

"Have a seat, Jeff," he said, motioning to a chair. I took a deep breath and complied. He looked me straight in the eye and said, "You're a great employee. You're doing a good job, and I'm confident that you'll have a long career here." My jaw dropped and I stared in disbelief. He actually praised me!

As I walked out of his office, all my "manning up" had done me no good when it came to processing his praise. He'd thrown me a curve ball that I wasn't prepared for, and tears filled my eyes.

I frantically wiped my face, not wanting anyone there to see me crying. His words and my reaction to them had me in a state of shock. I had no idea that his affirmation meant so much to me. It reached down into my core and touched some need that I thought had been neutralized.

* * * * *

How do you respond to affirmations from others? Have you neutralized the need for such words too, or do you thrive on them? Why do you think that is? Look back over your life and answer these questions, then ask the Lord to give you His perspective.

Father, it's so easy for us to want to please others and earn their affirmation. And while doing that isn't necessarily wrong, help us to be careful that we don't sin in the process or look to others for our value. Our worth comes from you alone.

Working from Both Sides of the Desk

Soon after this evaluation, I was promoted to supervisor. The pressure hit me like a ton of bricks. I began to understand the difficulties that my former supervisors navigated. If an employee didn't make their quota, they would get written up by their manager. After five write-ups, a one-day suspension was earned. More write-ups meant stiffer penalties. But ultimately, the stiffer penalties fell right back on the supervisor.

You see, by now the union had negotiated deal after deal until it was almost impossible now for non-managers to be fired. This meant the threat of non-managerial employees being fired was no longer in play. However, unlike the employees he oversaw, a supervisor could be fired. This put me, as a new supervisor, on a tightrope. The guys I oversaw could make or break me.

At the same time, I had learned a lot from my former supervisors. They each had a different style, yet I gained something from every one of them. I was able to experience both sides of the truth of John 15:15: "No longer do I call you slaves, for the slave does not know what his master is doing; but I have called you friends" (NASB). I had lived the difference. People who feel like servants or slaves only do what they have to do, but friends will want to do much more than what's required. As an hourly employee, I had worked as both. Now I was faced with applying those truths to find my own style of management.

I attempted to do the things that had meant so much to me when I was a new employee, and to avoid the things that had wrecked my confidence. The first step was to build trust. So I quickly developed friendships with the employees in my department. I got to know them and let them get to know me, I rolled up my sleeves and tried to walk with my team as they learned the tricks of the trade that I could pass on, and I determined to be a voice of encouragement and to show support and respect at every opportunity I could.

To my relief, it didn't take long for my new team to respond. They seemed to like being at work, and from all appearances they liked me. They worked so hard that before I knew it, my department performance numbers were up. My percentage of effectiveness rating was consistently 115 percent of the set quotas. That meant that if my managers set a goal of 1,000 boxes an hour, my team would have sorted 1,150 boxes in that hour. It is hard to imagine how much harder they had to work to accomplish that, but they did it because of relationship. I had respect for them, and they developed respect for me. I trusted them, and they trusted me.

That was the fun part of being a supervisor. Unfortunately, though I developed a good rapport with my team, I also learned that I couldn't always be their buddy. Difficult moments arose when I would have to confront them and hold their feet to the fire.

Though it was my least-favorite aspect of the job, I got a glimpse of the power of mutual respect. If I could begin talking with them about a performance issue by finding a place of appreciation for their other efforts, I would usually see walls go down, and they would generally be able to hear what I was saying. You see, I remembered what it felt like to sit on the other side of that desk.

Not long after I became supervisor, I was warned that a pretty big "challenge" was headed my way. Other supervisors said, "Hey, I hear that Joe is transferring into your department. Buckle up." When I asked what was wrong with Joe, they just replied, "Oh, you'll find out soon enough."

Upon further investigation, I learned that Joe had been moved from department to department and had the reputation of being an absolute nightmare. He was so difficult to work with that upper management had actually tried to fire him, but the union had gotten his job back, and the only recourse now was to move him. I was his next rotation.

We clashed right away. The chip on his shoulder out-weighed the largest of the boxes coming down that conveyor belt. We existed like this for a couple of weeks, and then one day when I asked him to do something, he lashed out, "Hey! Get away from me! I ain't gonna do that!"

Shocked, I decided to walk down to where he was. I knew he was volatile, so I asked him questions but tried to maintain a respectful tone. I was hoping to convey that I wanted to try to understand him. He continued to answer in a rough and defensive tone. I determined to remain calm and focused but tried to listen carefully. "I'm not trying to attack you here, Joe," I said. "I'm just trying to ask you what's going on."

As I continued asking him questions, he became less defensive and more approachable. I think when he finally realized that I was not attacking him and coming against him, he softened. "Jeff, I appreciate that, man," he said. "I really appreciate it. And I'm really sorry."

His whole attitude flipped in that moment. After bowing up and resisting me at every turn, he started looking for ways to do whatever needed to be done. I realized that in that relatively brief exchange, he saw that I was talking to him as a person and not as the "outcast" of second shift. He had experienced everyone else seeing him as a troublemaker, so it threw him when I treated him with respect. When he finally understood that I was on his side, he got on my side.

That experience ended up changing his path at UPS. He eventually was promoted to a highly respected full-time position, which was a job that he had been hoping for—and most importantly, he and I became and have remained friends.

* * * * *

Even in the good stuff—during the good times when things were beginning to go my way—I still missed what the Lord was trying to show me about how I am loved and valued by Him. So basing life on my experiences, I found myself believing …

- If I work hard, I will succeed.
- Since I have success, I am now valuable.
- If I work hard enough, I will be accepted.
- Performance is crucial to my being accepted.
- If I can perform well, I have worth.

Father, please reveal to me any place in my life where I am performing to receive your love. I confess the lie that my success and value in your eyes is connected to my performance. Help me receive the truth that I am loved simply for who I am, not for what I do.

4

How to Fail at Business
without Really Trying

Time seemed to pass slowly at UPS, but looking back on it now, I think it passed all too quickly. The early days were physically over-whelming, and the days of management were extremely stressful. My team was the largest, with thirty workers to manage. So every day was filled the intense realization of the guiding principle "No numbers, no job."

Though I was fortunate to have a team that genuinely tried to excel and have my back as a supervisor, the day-in and day-out stresses, both physically and mentally, took a toll on me. I was now twenty-one years old and exhausted, inside and out. I had maintained a grueling schedule of work-school-study, work-school-study day in and day out for years. As a result, my body and attitude began to show the wear.

By this time, I was in my third year of college, and my uncle, who is a physician, made a deal with me. He told me that as long as I kept up my grades, he would pay for my apartment but only four months at a time. That way our agreement could be tightly monitored. If I didn't keep my grades up, he would stop paying for my apartment. He was a wise man indeed. My intent was to keep my grades up because I was in pre-med classes and was set on achieving my goal of becoming a doctor just like my uncle. So I wholeheartedly agreed.

I found myself in an entirely new environment, and even though I had an intense schedule, I had more freedom. But I was running out of steam. People started talking about my heavy eyelids, bloodshot eyes, and lethargic attitude. Often these comments came from authorities and influencers in my life, and they began questioning my activities. Accusations of drug use soon surfaced. I could not seem to find anyone who really had my back and understood how hard I was trying to succeed and to measure up. But no one seemed to care whether my statements of innocence were true or not. I was summed up, accused, and judged. Court adjourned.

My engine began to sputter. After a while, I stopped defending myself and embraced the old adage "If you can't beat 'em, join 'em." I reasoned, *If they're accusing me anyway, I might as well be doing the thing they're accusing me of.* And that's when I began to party.

I had my own place and found friends who knew how to have a good time, and we had a blast. My apartment became party central. After a while, the inevitable happened and my grades started to drop. *But that's okay*, I reasoned. *I can afford to pay my own rent.*

One night, the party was going strong and I was on top of

the world. My friends and I were partying hard. Later that night, I fell asleep and slept hard and long—too long, in fact. I needed to be at a training session at work the next morning. But I slept right through it. Didn't show up, didn't even call. Truthfully, I had no phone. It wasn't in the budget, so I couldn't have called, even if I had deemed it important, which I did not. I didn't know it at the time, but I was on my way to learning some valuable lessons.

When I woke up and realized what had happened, I decided that I really didn't care about the consequences. Let them fire me. I had been thinking about quitting anyway. I had worked at UPS for five years, and that would give me a stellar reference so I could get a job anywhere.

When I arrived the next day, my coworkers had been looking for me for twenty-four hours. They were genuinely so concerned that they had called the local hospitals and my family members to see if I had been in an accident. I had never done this before, so they were frightened. When I strutted in unruffled, they invited me into the office. And the games began.

Though as a supervisor they could easily fire me, the procedure was to play a little mental game with the offender, which this time was me. I knew the way it worked. I had been trained in it. I was determined that they were not going to get to me. Not this time. So let the threats and mind tricks roll! Which they did.

"It will be a long time before we forget this!" they yelled among other threats.

I was braced and ready. Dripping with arrogance, I said, "Fine. I quit." I thought, *I'll be able to get a job anywhere. I don't have to take this. I'll show you!* And I got up and began to walk out.

The whole place was stunned and quiet. Everyone had heard what was going on. As I was leaving, someone ran over from the other side of the warehouse. He went into the office and shouted at management, "Please tell me you didn't just let Dollar go! You go after him! Don't do this!"

"What's it to you?" management demanded.

"He's one of your best!" was the answer. And the situation escalated to the point that as the guy kept on, management threatened to fire him. "Go ahead," he said, "I'll be happy to collect an unemployment check. But you've just made a big mistake."

As I was leaving the warehouse, I recognized the "someone" but couldn't believe my eyes. It was my first supervisor. The one who almost broke me. I found out that in addition to working at UPS, this man had been putting himself through law school—and he had a family to support. But as poignant a revelation as this was, I just kept walking.

* * * * *

As I learned to put more and more confidence in my flesh, my belief system did not improve. You can see how a type of an emotional "filtration system" was developing. I began believing …

- Success is up to me, and I know how to get it.
- I don't need anyone or anyone's help.
- I will be fine by myself.

Father, I confess the lie that I can only rely on myself, and that placing all confidence on my ability is pride. Scripture says that you resist the proud but give grace to the humble. I choose to humble myself now to receive your truth.

Dark Days Ahead

I had no idea that this was the beginning of a season of dark days for me. Try as I might, I could not find a job. Of course, I didn't try right away because I had a bit of severance pay and I thought it would be a piece of cake to find another employer. I thought I'd be a shoo-in. Other people had done it, and I was certain I would find a position that would probably be much better than what I had at UPS anyway.

I was wrong. All I could find were odd jobs. I worked as a night security guard at a popular restaurant chain, but soon found out that the janitor received more respect than I was given. Then I worked at a couple of different restaurants and tried some other odd jobs. Nothing was working out for me.

Finally, I found a job as a puller for a grocery distribution company. That meant at night and on Sundays, I would go in and suit up for pulling box after box out of the industrial refrigerator and freezer to load on a truck to distribute to local grocery stores for their Monday deliveries. I worked there for a year and earned a week of vacation.

One of the things that I have not yet addressed was my spiritual condition at this time. It probably won't shock you to know that I was not in a good place spiritually. I was raised in a traditional church where rules and regulations were expected to be followed. When you obeyed the rules, your soul was safe. Church attendance was imperative if you wanted a relationship with God. I began to fall away, and because of my new job, I stopped going to church—and then I began to grow my hair out, the ultimate rebellion! I had turned into a bona fide hippy.

My life during those years was filled with two things: work and partying. It was a way to numb out my reality. I couldn't admit to anyone how much I regretted leaving UPS. I didn't want to admit it to myself. I had an incredible future there. High-level management had told me that I was cut out for advancement at UPS and that there were opportunities available where the company would pay for me to finish college. I would be set up for a lucrative career if I wanted it. I guess I didn't really give it serious thought. Maybe I figured it would be there when I got ready for it. Either way, to think about what I had given up was debilitating. So I didn't. Day in and day out, I just tried to deaden the pain of regret and failure.

But I learned that one thing I could never deaden was that persistent yearning to be back in relationship with God. As much as I tried to ignore it, I couldn't. But the belief system I had at the time told me I was so far out of God's reach that I needed to walk down an aisle so I could pray with a preacher. I was stuck. For a year, I worked on Sundays and could not get to church.

* * * * *

The construction of my belief system continued:

- I am not only a failure, but also a stupid one.
- If I hide my regrets, I'll look strong and get respect from those in my community.
- I can divert inner pain if I can distract myself with "fun."

Perhaps you recognize places in your life where this is happening to you as well. If so, pray the prayer below with me.

Father, help me to see the places in my life where I am distracting myself in order to avoid pain. Lord, I confess that I've been using other things (fun, work, TV, internet, busyness, etc.) to distract me from my need for you. Please reveal to me the plans that you have for my life, to heal my pain.

The Dawn

Finally, I had earned a whole week of vacation. During that week, an unusual thing happened. Midweek, as I sat in front of the TV drinking alone, I happened to flip to a station where a television evangelist was making an extraordinary attempt to raise money. His gimmick was out there, and for some reason, it infuriated me. It hit me as so wrong and lit something in me, and I started yelling at the screen, "That's not right! That's not how it's supposed to be done!" I continued my rant with an array of miscellaneous expletives, so angry that I could have thrown something at the TV.

Then, as clear as a bell, I heard the Lord say, "Jeff?"

Everything in me stopped. I knew beyond a shadow of a doubt that I had just heard God's voice, but how could He be talking to me? I was a sinner. I thought He didn't have anything to do with sinners, and certainly not one who deserted Him for a lifestyle of partying and debauchery.

"I need some help," He continued.

It was unmistakable. I had just heard the voice of the Lord! But how could a Holy God have anything to do with a sinner like me? On top of that, this Holy God was *pursuing* me! At the time, this made no sense. According to my spiritual calculations, I had been the one who deserted Him. Therefore, according to this logic, I should be the one to return to Him. I had no paradigm for Him pursuing me, instead thinking I had to pursue Him to get back in His good graces.

I knew what I had to do. Right then and there, I made a fervent promise to the Lord: "Okay, I'll go back to church, but you know that the only chance I have to get to church for another year is this Sunday."

"Just show up," He responded.

I promised God I would go back to church on Sunday and get myself right with Him. I was cautiously optimistic. Could I really put my trust in the conversation I just had? And more importantly than that, could I really put my trust in Him? I was tired of the emptiness of the life I was leading and wondered if I would truly find my way back.

Unfortunately, my return to Him was short-lived. I picked right back up where I left off, continuing to party. The conversation dissipated, and surprisingly I forgot about it. I enjoyed the rest of my vacation time and got with some of my friends as usual. I was determined to blow it out on the last weekend of my vacation, and so were my friends. We ended up going out Saturday night and partying. We were having so much fun that I never even thought once about my promises to God. I got home at five in the morning, fell asleep, and didn't wake up until five that afternoon.

When I woke up, I called my friends to see if they wanted to continue our weekend fun, but every one of them had other plans. I thought, *Wow, this is weird. This never happens with these guys.* Then out of the clear blue, I heard the Lord's voice again: "Jeff, I thought you said that you were going to go to church."

I gasped—I had totally forgotten my promise! I was so frustrated. This was my only Sunday off in a year, with none in sight for another full twelve months. "You know what?" I said to Him. "You're absolutely right. I did tell you that." I looked at the clock and saw that I had just enough time to make the evening service.

On the way to the church that night, I kept envisioning my walk down the aisle to peace and freedom. I knew what I had said yes to: coming back to Him and forsaking my lifestyle and my ways. I even knew that this decision could cost me my friendships, and I was okay with that. I was tired and desperate.

However, things didn't quite go as I planned. That night was the church's annual missions night, and it was the only service all year without an altar call.

I was devastated. I couldn't believe it. Of all the Sundays to go to church, I picked this one. I thought I was done—locked into this lifestyle for another year! I was so looking forward to relief, and now that relief was out of my reach. I felt like I had messed up so badly and the door to the Lord was shut. I had finally turned my heart toward Him again, but I couldn't get back in.

Even though I realized I had screwed up my life and knew I didn't measure up, I still had a deep yearning to be right with God. After church that night, I told one of my Christian friends, "Don't ever leave the church—ever!" I left him in the parking lot of the church that night not knowing how to help me. He could see me crying as I got into my car.

I left church completely devastated. The next day would begin another year of misery for me, and it would be twelve months before I would have the same chance to go to church. I felt trapped and didn't know any way out.

Fortunately, my Christian friends knew how devastated I was, and one of them had a brother in seminary who heard what had happened in the church parking lot and offered to come over and pray with me. I determined that since he was a seminary student, he would qualify as someone with enough spiritual knowledge to pray for me to come back into the flock. I was so hopeful.

We prayed together that night, and I was flooded with God's peace. His goodness overwhelmed me. I can't describe how wonderful it felt to be back! It felt so good, in fact, that the very next day I quit my job and committed to faithfully attending church again.

* * * * *

Have you ever experienced a time when you believed that you heard something from the Lord and you disobeyed it? I want to encourage you that God is faithful and that He is the God of the "second chance."

Thank you, Father, that you are faithful and that you never leave us or forsake us.

God's Gift

My desire to serve the Lord and be back in His "good graces" again was finally being fulfilled. I felt like my heart was home. No more running. No more hiding. No more fighting. I felt such relief, such peace.

I started hanging out with new friends. My activities changed. The wild parties at my apartment were replaced by prayer meetings and Bible studies. One night my friends and I went to a Christian concert, and through a group of mutual friends, I met a very special person. At the time I didn't know it, but I had just been introduced to my future wife, Becky.

Anyone who has seen my beautiful wife would have a hard time believing me when I say that when I first met her, all I saw was Jesus. But it is absolutely true. There was something so different about her. This young woman had a passion for the Lord like I had never seen. We soon became friends, and one day I invited her to come to the Bible study/prayer group we held at my apartment. She agreed, with the condition that I would be willing go to hers as well, and I was all in.

On the evening that Becky came to my Bible study, she captivated the group. We all took turns talking about our lives and what we were processing about God and ourselves, with each person speaking and commenting on their own individual progress and the progress of others. We were encouraging each other's walk with the Lord. However, I noticed something unusual about Becky. When she would speak, a hush would come over the room. No one else was even tempted to talk. There was something so different about her. She didn't take over the conversation, she simply commented about how the Lord had been so real and tangible to her. All I can say is that Jesus radiated from her. I wanted whatever it was that she had. The yearning I had inside was legitimized. There was more of God available, and I had to have it.

The day came for me to attend Becky's Bible study, and I found myself at a small Episcopal church. I had no big expectations but was curious to see Becky's spiritual environment, and this was one of the places she frequented. I had no idea what was in store for me.

Becky and I walked in and sat down. About forty people were there that night, and we sang worship songs that I was not familiar with, but I was up for learning new songs. Then a woman got up to give the message. Her keen knowledge of the Bible stunned me. I remember thinking, *I wonder what concordance she is using. Where did she find these truths? This is amazing!* The more I listened, the more I was blown away. I thought, *Who in the world is this woman?* I had never heard such things, but my soul was deeply stirred.

After her teaching, the woman asked if anyone needed ministry. She invited anyone who needed healing in their body to come forward. Shocked, I thought, *Wow! They're doing the "stuff"!* Then she gave an invitation to anyone who was wanting to come and receive the power of the Holy Spirit.

I asked Becky, "What is that?" She tried to answer, but before she could, I asked, "Is it tongues?" My church had frowned upon this.

Becky answered, "No, not necessarily."

"Do you have it?" I asked.

"Yes."

"That's it," I decided. "That's what I'm missing."

Becky asked if I wanted to go up and get prayer. I waited until everyone left and then found myself standing before the woman. As she prayed, I felt something go from the top of my head down to the bottom of my feet and then go back up again. It was like liquid honey or something. I couldn't explain it, but it was amazing.

In that moment, my life was changed. This was the most fantastic thing I could have ever imagined. I had known there was more, and now I was experiencing it. I hadn't realized that "this" was what I had been looking for. I couldn't wait to share it with all my friends. It was the most exciting discovery I had ever known.

The next week at my Bible study, with childlike enthusiasm and unbridled zeal, I shared my newfound revelation with everyone. And I mean everyone. However, astonishingly, not everyone shared the same enthusiasm for my experience. In fact, I unintentionally caused a bit of a stir in some circles in my church. After a few months of my continued "enthusiasm," they eventually asked me to find another place to share these amazing revelations. They were tender and respectful toward me in their request, and so was I toward them. No animosity or resentment came between us; I simply complied and left.

It was a confusing time for me. I did not realize it then, but the Lord was directing my steps toward my destiny and purpose.

* * * * *

Though my life was changing in radical ways, my belief system was still flawed. Deep down I believed …

- My opinion will be judged.
- My convictions are not important.
- Even when I try to do right, I will still be rejected.
- No matter how hard I try, I still will not measure up.

Father, please forgive me for the believing the lie that my opinions will be judged and I will be rejected because of my beliefs. I recognize that even though it's important to confess our faults/beliefs/sins to God, it is equally important to forgive others who have hurt us. I choose to forgive those who have judged and rejected me.

Married with Children

Time passed, and by God's grace and mercy, the friendship between Becky and me deepened. I could now call this beautiful woman who radiated Jesus (and still does) my wife. That part of my life was going very well. Unfortunately, all my efforts as a provider seemed lacking, and the deck still seemed like it was stacking up higher and higher.

Our world was turned upside down when our first baby, our little girl, Bethany, was born two months premature. She weighed two and a half pounds at birth. We were terrified we would lose her. The newborn intensive care unit (NICU) was all she knew for the first two months of her life. Day in and day out, our little girl was poked and prodded—all in a valiant attempt to save her life, but she was still traumatized. We felt helpless in our separation from her until our prayers were finally answered and she was strong enough (at a whopping five pounds) to come home.

We were elated when we brought her home, with hopes

of a normal life ahead and hospital days behind us. Just the fact that our little girl was strong enough to be in her new home was such a relief to us. However, I underestimated how difficult the transition would be for her. She had never had the opportunity to sleep for more than a couple hours at a time due to all the tests and examinations that were necessary for her to survive. It took Bethany two years to sleep through the night.

Becky, however, was a trooper. I was traumatized. The slightest noise would terrify our baby, and because of the trauma, she would cry and scream. To make matters worse, we lived by the airport. Like clockwork every morning, no matter how short the night, Bethany would awaken with a jolt when that first jet took off. Becky had the patience of a saint, but I wanted to fix everything for my wife and baby and felt absolutely powerless to do so.

The one thing I knew I could do was work. I consistently worked at least two and sometimes three jobs. I had to. You see, we didn't have medical insurance. Our first medical bill was $89,000—and that was just for NICU. We were numb and overwhelmed. When the hospital called to set us up on a payment plan, the payment was as much as our rent. Paying it was impossible.

It didn't take long for us to be turned over to collections, and their agencies called relentlessly. The pressure was overwhelming. I was trying to manage it as best I could, but it seemed like I was always failing again. However, Becky was a tower of strength and hope. Even in the intensity, she was an amazing nurturer to our little girl. She also began handling most of the calls from the collection agencies, fronting them while I was working. We ended up paying what we could, though it was a small amount in the eyes of our creditors.

Even though those times were tough, I look back on them

with appreciation. Yes, I'm glad we survived them, and I also want to declare that there is no amount of money in existence that could equal the love and gratitude I have for my daughter.

Those times were also rich with testimonies of God's faithfulness. Time after time, our needs were supernaturally met. We were and still are a part of a community of strong believers that walked with us during those trying times. I also know that the hard times we went through are cakewalks in comparison to so many other people's stories. My intention here is to illustrate the continual building of the infrastructure that was going on inside me even though I did not have a clue that it was happening. Not yet anyway.

* * * * *

My belief system was screaming at me by now:

- I am a failure.
- I am a failure as a provider.
- I must not be pleasing God.
- I have to try harder to succeed in God's eyes.
- I know God loves me, but I don't think He likes me.

Father, help me to believe your truth even when the facts and circumstances in my life appear different from what you've promised. Even though I can't see it now, I choose to trust you.

Letting Others Win

One of the jobs that I worked for many years was as a server at a high-end restaurant. I was extremely grateful for that opportunity because at the end of my evening shift, I would have enough cash to stop by the store and pick up formula and diapers on my way home. There were other reasons I appreciated working there as well. The job involved a measure of stress, as any job does, but I was able to interact with people and facilitate an atmosphere of enjoyment. I often earned a little extra of those much-needed tips by being attentive to my customers.

Some people say I have a pretty good sense of humor. I don't know if they are right or not, but I sure do enjoy a good laugh. That should probably be attributed to my grandfather and my uncles; they are some of the funniest people I have ever known. I tried to keep up with them at family gatherings, but to no avail. There was no use in trying to one-up them. I would have done much better to just take notes. Either way, I am grateful to come from a family that appreciates humor. Usually, this worked to my benefit in my job as a server.

If I sensed a customer had a good sense of humor, I took advantage of the opportunity and attempted to interject some humor into the conversation. Who wouldn't want a good laugh, right? My problem was that I didn't know when to stop. As a result, I would one-up people in trying to be funny. Unfortunately, I didn't realize that my identity was a bit too involved, and I couldn't discern when enough was enough—and too much stinks.

One night, I had a hint that my view was off when a customer gave me some advice that I did not expect. Business professionals often reserved private dining rooms that the restaurant offered, and on this particular evening, a pharmaceutical representative hosted a dinner for a dozen or so doctors to give a presentation about his products. The dinner went well, and the host gave me a nice tip, so I assumed he was happy with my service. However, I noticed that he was hanging around after his guests had all left.

Before I had a chance to ask him if there was anything else he needed, he asked, "Can I speak to you for a second?"

"Sure," I responded.

"I can tell that you're a really good guy, so I wanted to mention something to you that I'm pretty sure you don't realize." Lowering his voice, he continued, "In fact, I know you don't realize it. You did a good job with our service. It was great. But ... you came across as a bit of a smart aleck."

I was horrified. "Oh no! I am so sorry!" I had thought my bantering with him and his customers was my being friendly and humorous, but they had seen it as being cocky and insensitive.

He could see that I was rattled, so he said kindly but firmly,

"I know you don't see yourself as coming across to people like that. That's why I thought you needed to know." He was calm and didn't seem upset with me, and I sensed that he knew he was giving me revelatory advice.

"Wow, thank you for telling me this," I said. "You're right. I had no idea."

I tried to apologize again, but he emphasized, "It isn't a big deal, but I thought you ought to know." In his tone was the awareness that this information was going to sting but it would be worth it if I got the message. And I sure did—or at least I thought I did. Still, it took God sending someone else to really hammer the point home.

Around Christmastime, not surprisingly our busiest time of the year, I was serving a group of employees who worked for a small business, and the owner was honoring them by hosting a dinner at our fine restaurant. This business owner was polite, kind, and in an overall jovial mood. He started joking around with his employees and interacting with me as well. Tonight was his night, and this was a well-earned reward for a great year.

This company was clearly a fun place to work. Everyone's spirits were high, and the atmosphere was enjoyable and lively. The evening progressed wonderfully. We were all getting along and having lots of laughs and playful banter—or so I thought.

As the meal progressed, I noticed a change in the host's demeanor. Instead of joking with me, he was simply polite. By the end of the evening, the entire group seemed a bit subdued. It didn't take a genius to surmise that I had done something that had caused this awkwardness.

Soon my suspicions were confirmed. The owner of the restaurant called me into his office. This had never happened before, and I had no idea what it might mean. As soon as I sat down, he dropped a bomb on me: "I just got a phone call from Mr. Galloway, and he told me you were his waiter. He said that he has been coming to our restaurant for years and has always enjoyed it. Jeff, he then told me that he would continue to come back to this restaurant under one condition: that you are never his server again. And as a matter of fact, he demanded that we put that into our records on our computer to ensure that his request be honored."

I felt like someone had punched me in the stomach.

"This man is furious," the owner added.

My mind raced to comprehend what I was hearing. *How could this have happened? How could he be furious with me?* I had thought all along that he was having a good time. Actually, I thought we were all having a good time. I could not figure out what happened that caused things to go so terribly wrong. There were no inappropriate words. None of them had too much to drink. I thought he enjoyed me "helping" to liven things up at the table.

"I am so sorry! I am so, so sorry!" The words spurted out of my mouth, as I knew nothing else to say. It was hard to come to grips with the fact that I had offended someone so deeply that he would take the time to call the restaurant owner and insist that I never be his server again.

Justifiably, I braced for the dreaded words "You're fired," but thankfully, my boss had no intention of letting me go.

"Jeff, you have this ability to go further than just about any-body can go with humor. I have never seen anything like it. When it comes to joking around, you can go as far and keep up with almost everybody," he explained. "But the thing you don't realize is that sometimes you just need to let other people win." He continued, "You never let others win. I know you don't realize that you're coming across like this, but it seems like you always have to one-up everyone else's humor."

This painful moment was a real paradigm shift for me. I remembered how the pharmaceutical rep had said that I came across as a smart aleck. Now I had just embarrassed a business owner in front of his employees by taking the bantering to a derogatory level. Further, the owner of the restaurant was telling me that I came across as someone who had to trump everyone else. I was floored when I got a glimpse of how other people saw me. My interactions came across completely opposite of the way I intended them.

Grateful that I wasn't fired, I left his office humbled and remorseful. I was determined to change. I evaluated how I interacted with my customers and sought advice from servers who had more experience than I did and were evidently doing something right because their tips were consistently better than mine. I decided that this time I would listen.

Their message to me was surprisingly simple: "You don't need to entertain your customers. You just need to serve them well. The better the service, the better the tips." After hearing this, I realized I was actually taking the attention away from the customer and putting it on me.

I learned some valuable lessons that day. Soon my service became more about the customer instead of about me. As I gained finesse in engaging with the customer enough to make them feel welcome but making the main focus serving them well, I received positive feedback and my tips improved as well.

In pondering whether or not to include this experience

in this book, I wondered if my propensity for one-upping might be connected to the need to be right. It seems that both are an attempt for personal affirmation. In other words, "an affirmation for me at the cost of affirmation for you." Proverbs says it so well: "Senseless people find no pleasure in acquiring true wisdom, for all they want to do is impress you with what they know" (Proverbs 18:2 TPT).

I have noticed that people often seem to want to one-up each other. In casual conversation, I've seen how people, in an attempt to connect, fall into the trap of trying to overshadow each other. It's unintentional perhaps, but still the end result is the same. Someone usually feels devalued. Conversation shouldn't be a competition. It should be a means to grow in relationship with each other.

Just this week, a person was talking to me about a mistake he had made, and the way he told it made the story take a funny turn. I responded by telling a story with a similarly humorous slant, but soon I could sense that he thought mine came across as funnier than his. Although my intention was to use humor to be relational, he felt overshadowed by my story and felt that it was outshining his. That caused him to feel a bit shut down, like he had taken a backseat in a conversation that *he* started.

God checked my heart and posed this question to me: "Why can't a person say something funny and you not add to it?"

I thought, *I'm doing it again, aren't I?* When God brought that question to my mind, I remembered what I had learned at the restaurant years before. Why couldn't that same principle of serving a customer be applied in conversation to a friend?

The Lords says, "Those who possess wisdom don't feel the need to impress others with what they know, but foolish ones make sure their ignorance is on display" (Proverbs 12:23 TPT). Could it be that when someone's identity is in Jesus—who is Wisdom, and the True Lover of their souls—the driving desire to have their significance affirmed by man would dissipate?

An Adjustment Is Needed

We were designed for community. Therefore, building enduring relationships is crucial for our well-being. My point here is for us to learn how to truly celebrate others who are in our lives and to also learn how to listen and discern the things that are valuable and important to them. So, even in the face of our day-to-day stresses, the urgencies, and the frustrations that life often holds, we should dial down, pause, and simply remember who we are in Jesus and the call we have upon our lives. We should also remember that every good work He has called us to do was already written down before we breathed our first breath on this earth.

I don't want to miss the opportunity to accomplish each one of the good works God has called me to do. I also think that those good works might start more simply than we think. Maybe if we slowed down and learned how to listen to the Holy Spirit with a heart committed to truly loving others as He loves us, our knee-jerk response would soon be to genuinely listen to the hearts of others and learn how to honor and celebrate those God has placed in our lives.

* * * * *

Even though I was gaining revelation from the Lord, my belief system (ungodly beliefs) was still based on lies:

- I am not enough.
- I have to be likable for approval and affirmation.
- I have to perform to be accepted.
- I have to be the best or I have no worth.

Do you ever find yourself trying to one-up others? Or did you realize, while reading this chapter, that this is something you unintentionally do? If so, determine to take care in your interactions with people in the future.

Father, help us to discern the best way to interact with others. Sometimes it's so easy to talk about ourselves, so give us the wisdom to know when to listen and when to speak.

Dealing with Your Two Percent

My young family was growing. We were thrilled to celebrate the birth of our baby boy. My family was and is my delight and the most important thing in my world. Having said that, even with as much of my heart as they held, I felt something was not complete.

My desire to be in ministry was burning within me. In some ways, I felt trapped. The financial pressure was definitely a burden, but that wasn't driving my discontentment. There was an ache in my heart that I carried around. It seemed like who I was and what I did were not congruent. I had a deep yearning to be in ministry and yet saw no avenue to get there. At church, I was on the ministry team and praying for people, and I loved sharing the Lord with others and watching their lives change as He showed up. It was what helped bridge that longing in my heart.

I remembered, when I was six or seven years old, being asked by our pastor's wife what I wanted to be when I grew up. I chuckle now when I remember my answer. "I think I'll probably be a song leader," I told them, "because I don't really think I would like to be a pastor because I don't think I would want to talk every week. I just don't think I could say something every week." I realized that, even at that young age, I felt a call to be in some form of ministry.

This doesn't mean that I think everyone who has a call on their lives needs to be in some type of organized ministry. We are all called to represent Jesus on this earth. He uses our individual giftings, talents, and desires to place His people all over the world in all spheres of life. I just knew that, somehow, I needed to be in a different place, but had no idea how to get there. I kept hitting an impenetrable wall that had no doors, and was desperately trying find an opening somewhere.

I watched as several of my friends had doors of opportunity miraculously open for them. I wondered what my problem was. Why was God not opening doors for me? Did He not know my desires? Did He not know that I desired to be in ministry? Why was I so stuck? Why wasn't He helping me? I had no idea at the time that He was about to give me an answer to all these questions.

Even though this inner discontentment was churning in my heart, my external life continued moving right along. I still needed to work two jobs to make ends meet, but I had a healthy community of friends who were walking with me through these times—friends who would speak honestly to support me, encourage me, and, if necessary, point out my shortcomings, for which I was extremely grateful.

Another thing I was grateful for was a new job. My new boss happened to be a Christian, and he gave me this job right when I needed it. He seemed like such a great guy, and things were going along really well. We went to the same church, and at work we were able to comment on the message we'd heard that Sunday. It was like a breath of fresh air for me. It was so nice to have another believer in the workplace. My work life seemed to be going great.

That is, until the day we had an altercation. He completely lost it, and lost it on me. I didn't know that he had a rage problem, but I soon found out. He called me into his office and proceeded to give me the most public chiding I had ever received—ever.

I had never experienced anything like this before, even in my UPS days! He was explosive, and his anger kept escalating until his verbal assault was unbearable. I understood my employee rights from past management experience, and I knew I did not have to sit there while he was berating me with such explosive hostility. I decided the best thing for me to do was to remove myself from the onslaught. "I don't have to take this," I said as I walked out of his office.

As I was walking down the hallway, my boss continued his tirade, ranting and yelling, "If you walk out of here, this is insubordination!"

By this time, the whole office could hear him. Doors began to fly open as other managers stuck their heads out of their offices to see what was going on. They could not help but hear what my boss was saying because his voice echoed down the hallway. As I continued leaving, all I could do was ask them, "Are you hearing this? Are you hearing the way he's talking to me? Can you believe this guy?" I was secretly hoping someone was recording it.

I left, overwhelmed, confused, and belittled, and went straight to talk to my friend who was an elder in our church. I wanted some insight and a godly perspective because I was spinning like crazy. I still couldn't get my mind around what had just happened, and I knew my friend would have wise counsel. I was desperate for help.

I explained the situation to him. Being a business owner himself, he was shocked at my boss's reaction and extremely supportive to me. "Wow. That's terrible, Jeff," he said empathetically. "Man, I'm sorry this happened to you. That really was abusive. What an awful experience."

I wholeheartedly agreed. I thought, *Thank God that someone is finally able to see what I went through and what happened to me.* At last I felt somewhat vindicated in this situation, as this elder had deemed that it was absolutely not my fault. Finally, someone saw and understood that I was innocent and a victim here.

The Painful Realization

That next Sunday, my friend followed up with me. "Hey Jeff, I've been thinking about our conversation and that incident with your boss. I know that was a bad situation—actually, an awful one. However, I have been thinking about it all weekend, and, well, God's been kinda nudging me on something. So … let's just say that your boss was ninety-eight percent wrong, and it sounds like he definitely was. But even with that being true, and as bad as that was, I feel like the Lord is still concerned about your two percent. I think you might need to own your part in this, even if it's just a small percentage, and you might need to apologize to him."

Whoa! Wait a minute. You have got to be kidding me, I thought. *This can't be right. This isn't fair. If he's ninety-eight percent wrong, then if anything, he needs to come to me. He was the one who was out of control. He violated every rule of management. That man could get fired over the things he said to me, much less the way he said them. He was the rage-aholic. And I have witnesses. I just happened to be the one in his path at the moment he needed a human punching bag. I did nothing to provoke him.*

I could not get beyond the injustice of the victim having to apologize to the perpetrator. I was the one who needed counseling after the things he said. In my mind, the one who tipped the scales of justice needed to be the one who was responsible to correct them. However, as unfair as it felt, and as much as I did not want to hear it, deep down I knew it was the Lord speaking. I knew in my spirit that this was a direct word from God and that my friend was sharing God's heart for me in this matter.

This was a profound revelation for me. Gone were the days of score keeping. This new awareness began to dissolve the thoughts *He's the one who needs to apologize. He's the one who started this. If he treats me like this, then he deserves to be treated the same way.* My heart just sank. All night, I wrestled with this revelation, dreading what I had to do, but I knew that I was going to have to call this guy up and give him my apology.

The next day, as difficult as it was, I mustered up the courage and called my boss and apologized. It was not an offhand, casual apology either. I realized that I did not represent Jesus in that explosive exchange in his office and I needed to take responsibility for my response to him, so my apology was sincere. I told him I was sorry for the attitude I had toward him and my disrespectful actions. Though this was one of the harder things I had ever done, his response surprised me. The situation began to diffuse between us, and he actually apologized to me.

That was one of my first glimpses of the power of humility. When I made the decision to do what the Lord asked me to do, whether my emotions agreed or not, it made room for the Holy

Spirit to work on both of us. I could have argued with my boss and presented a winnable case in any court that he owed me an apology, but I would have never expected that he would have agreed. When I got out of the way and allowed the Lord to get involved in *His* way, He was able to touch my boss in a way that no human could. I eventually left that job, but the important thing for me was that I left on good terms instead of hostile terms. I was learning to be a peacemaker, and I was learning to own my mistakes, even the ones that seemed small and insignificant.

* * * * *

Though I was receiving godly revelation and instruction, I was still faltering with my belief system:

- I will always be misunderstood.
- There is no one on my side.
- Calamity will always follow me.

Have you ever noticed that the places that are your biggest areas of growth in life actually require more attention than you originally anticipated? Thanks be to God that He is continually conforming us to the image of Jesus.

11

The Big Question

One night, I had a dream that turned out to be one of the most simple yet powerful dreams of my life. In it, someone said, "Describe your life in one word." Before I could think, the word *unfulfilled* shot out of my mouth. I awoke completely bewildered.

The dream really rattled me. I hated to admit it, but it was true. I didn't want it to be true. Didn't I have everything that really mattered? I had a beautiful, loving wife who loves Jesus and people (and me) and radiates Him like no one I've ever known. I had my children, who are the delight of my heart. Yes, the financial struggles were there, but God continued showing Himself faithful, and our needs were being met, even if just barely.

What was wrong with me? I loved the Lord with my whole heart, at least the whole part of my heart that I knew. The only thing that made sense was that the deep longing to serve the Lord in ministry was so strong that it felt like I had a hole in my heart and nothing could come close to filling it except more of Him.

No new doors were opening anywhere for me and I felt stuck. It was as if there was a tension between the "now" and the "not yet" that I could do nothing about. Try as I might to ignore the discontentment, it was relentless. I felt the Lord had called me into ministry and then closed all the doors for me to get there. I even challenged my heart and wondered if these desires to be in ministry were selfish.

I didn't realize at the time that God *gives* us the desires of our heart. I knew Psalm 37:4: "Delight yourself in the Lord; and He will give you the desires of your heart" (NASB). But I didn't realize that His love for me was so profound that He literally works through the desires He gives us and that He actually gives us those desires in the first place. I thought I had gotten that wrong as well—at least where it applied to me. I probably wasn't delighting myself enough in the Lord. That would explain it. Another performance failure.

I was totally unaware that I believed my value as a person was set securely in what I did. How I performed life was everything, and though I couldn't see it, it was how I measured myself and felt others measured me as well. It was survival. I had a job to do, and that was to hide who I really was from everyone else. If we could measure self-worth, I felt that everyone else might have started at zero, but I started at about negative fifteen. I had to use extra energy and work incredibly hard just to get up to zero. If something good happened to me, if I met a new friend or got a promotion or someone gave me a compliment, I lived in fear of it just being a matter of time before they found out that they had the wrong guy.

I felt like I had to perform to be accepted—that I had to be the funniest, the most polite, the smartest, the most giving, the most caring, the best worker, and on and on. It was relentless and exhausting. I was striving desperately for acceptance because if I was not accepted, I would be rejected. For me, rejection meant utter abandonment and disgrace—a feeling of being completely discarded as the person I wanted to be. If people didn't like me, if I wasn't accepted, I simply had no value, and if I had no value, then what was the point? This was why I needed to fiercely protect myself by hiding who I really was, because deep in my heart, I knew I didn't measure up.

Turning a Deaf Ear

Unfortunately, this discontentment began to show up in my relationships and daily attitudes. I didn't know it. I couldn't see it. I couldn't hear it when a loved one tried to tell me. As you can see, I had set up this mental "filtration system" that filtered out my faults. It was a system created purely for my protection. In my mind, I had justifiable reasons for not trusting the people who were in a position to really know me. When they would try to point out my faults, their words would fall flat, and I would walk away unscathed and, most importantly, unknown. If I could hide who I really believed I was, I would be okay. I didn't realize that it is hard to hide who you really are from those who love you the most.

I became pretty good at working through this filtration system. When those closest to me tried to tell me something, I had an effective defense. I had a mental "caste" system that allowed me to place everyone in their appropriate place when they attempted to speak into my life. I would listen to people only if I deemed them important. If they had an impressive spiritual pedigree, an impactful testimony, or if they were successful or educated, then of course I would listen. I wanted to be all I could be in Him, and I knew if He sent someone special like that, then that person would have a special message for me directly from God.

But when Becky would mention to me that I might be a bit critical or a little touchy, I would disregard her remarks because I felt that she was just judging me. When my little Bethany would say, "Daddy, you're being mean to me," I would answer, "Honey, you're five years old. You're too young to understand what Daddy's going through right now. One day, when you're older, you'll understand what I mean."

Stuck in Life

At this time, I didn't realize that my life was stuck. I wasn't moving forward. It seemed like my life had been put on "pause," and it was during this time that my young family and I found ourselves attending a new church. We felt like the Lord had specifically directed us to leave our old church and attend this new one. So we did.

When we had been going there for several months, we arrived one Sunday to find that the church had done an outreach to some impoverished areas of our city that week and had invited these "unchurched" folks to visit. All kinds of new people were standing around outside when we got there. Some were smoking, some were dressed on the inappropriate side, some had shocking body piercings, and others had appalling tattoos. As we were walking in, all I could do was watch as my young children stared in curiosity at the new "guests" who were visiting.

The Setup

The service started like it did every week, but while everyone was singing worship songs, I was dwelling on my irritation with the leaders of the church, thinking that they should have managed that whole thing better. *Those people could have a bad influence on us—and not only on us but, more importantly, on our children!* I thought. *What were they thinking letting those people in? Can't the leaders see the potential harm this could do to our families? They've really missed it this time!* I was fuming. The whole time everyone was standing and worshiping, I was sitting down being angry and making judgments against the leaders.

That is, until God interrupted my judgments and said to me, "Jeff, what do you think my ministry looks like?"

"What do you mean, Lord?" I asked.

He answered, "Well, when it says in Scripture that Jesus was a friend of sinners, what do you think the 'sinners' looked like?"

I wrestled with this a bit but still wasn't moved. In my mind, I knew that Jesus' love was never isolated to certain social types. And I also knew that Jesus did not care about or judge or notice people's creative social expressions. He loved everyone, and I got that. However, my opinion still didn't change. I had a valid point, and in reality my heart was still afraid and embittered, so it was much easier to rest in the judgments.

I will never forget the next question God asked me: "Jeff, how would you know if you were wrong?"

His question surprised me. I tried to analyze what He was asking. I wanted to find a logical argument because the question seemed logical, and yet I found it so illogical that I couldn't give Him an immediate answer. "What do you mean, Lord?" I asked.

He asked another way: "What would it look like if you were wrong? In other words, pretend that you're in a movie and you're the director and the leading actor and the writer. Show me the cast of people who are around you, and set up the scene in which you would realize that you were wrong. What would that scene look like? Where would this scene take place? Who else would be there in the scene with you? Describe this scene and the characters."

I still wasn't following. I believed I was doing all the right things. You could ask anyone. I was a godly man. I attended church regularly. I worked hard to provide for my family. I tithed, I served, and when I prayed for people, the Lord showed up. For the most part, I was working so hard at doing the right things that if someone was going to be wrong in a given situation, I couldn't imagine it would be me.

So without hesitation, my answer was, "Lord, I would know I was in the wrong if I had a sense in my spirit that I was at fault. Or if you told me—or if you showed me in a dream or maybe had an angel visit me or something like that."

I couldn't believe the trouble I was having answering His simple question. My confusion was short-lived. Within seconds, God abruptly showed me three scenes in which different people in three of the main spheres of my life had approached me in the last week.

"Would it look like your boss telling you that he's noticed you had a bad attitude?" God asked. He now had my full attention. Just last week, my boss had called me into his office and spoken to me about my bad attitude that day. I remember thinking at the time, *I'm not the one with the bad attitude. You're the one with the attitude problem. As a matter of fact, no one really even wants to work for you.*

Before I could get my mind around that question, God fired another one at me: "Or would it look like Becky telling you that you're being short and irritable with her?" Sure enough, a few days earlier, Becky had told me that exact thing—that I was being short-tempered and testy with her. My response was full-blown denial and self-defense: "It's not me. I'm not being irritable. You're just being too sensitive, and actually, you're criticizing me."

Again, before I could process all that, God asked me another question: "Or would it look like little Bethany telling you that you're being too harsh with her?" I remembered the exact situation, again during that same week, when I had spoken to Bethany harshly, saying, "I've told you twenty-seven times, and you're just not listening to me!"

The Lord then grouped all these individual situations together, neatly presented this package to me, and said, "Now, would that look like you were wrong?"

When He asked me those three questions in rapid-fire succession and applied them to the real-life events from which they were birthed, I was taken down at the knees. A sudden awareness of all the finger-pointing I had done overwhelmed me. I realized, *Oh, dear God. It's not them, it's me! I'm the one who's wrong!*

The realization was paramount. The Lord had used three different people in my life to give me a message, but I didn't receive it because I had judged the messengers. I had considered them unreliable because I perceived them to have "flaws" or "handicaps" that would affect their ability to evaluate *me*.

What a revelation! I was getting a direct correction from the Lord, and it was something that I had never been aware of before. In hindsight, He was actively walking me through the parable of

Matthew 7 about the speck and the log. The Passion Translation puts it this way:

> "Why would you focus on the flaw in
> someone else's life and yet fail to notice
> the glaring flaws of your own? How could
> you say to your friend, 'Let me show you
> where you're wrong,' when you're guilty of
> even more? You're being hypercritical and
> a hypocrite! First acknowledge your own
> 'blind spots' and deal with them, and then
> you'll be capable of dealing with the 'blind
> spot' of your friend." (Matthew 7:3–5)

The people God had placed closest to me in my life were all giving me the same message, yet I could not receive it. They were giving me accurate feedback on how they were experiencing me, and I could not hear it. I had been *the* reason for my life being stuck, and the realization of this was overwhelming. I had been so keen in identifying other's "faults" and "defects" that I had overlooked my own.

This was amazing! God put His finger directly on the issue and showed me the issue *was* me. I couldn't believe it. This revelation was so powerful and transforming that since then, it's like the Lord has given me a new pair of glasses with lenses that show me the limit of my own perspective.

When Father God asked me these questions, it revolutionized my life. They are still revolutionizing my life to this day. This is a living revelation that breathes upon every event, every situation, and every age and stage of life. There is no place in life that this truth is not applicable.

The Revelation

Now let's take this to an even deeper level. Why was it so hard for me to be wrong? In thinking back, I can tell you it was a fight that was as desperate as the one for survival to live. Because my identity was based on my performance in life and the opinions of other people, if I was wrong, that meant I had no value, because I only possessed value if I was right.

But when the Lord showed me that He had placed people in my life and charged them to speak into my life, somehow I didn't understand that I was never intended to walk this pathway alone—that my flaws were not attached to *who* I was or they would be dealt with just between the Lord and me. I always believed God spoke to us through His Word, and that is true. What I didn't realize was that He also speaks through people, and, in my case, the ones who were the closest to me—my wife, my daughter, and even my boss. However, I didn't realize that we were created and designed to walk through this life with others, allowing them to be so intimately involved in our lives that a trust would develop—a trust that is strong enough to allow them to have access to our hearts and in turn for us to be able to *trust* them with our shortcomings.

God's questions are living wisdom. They are multi-dimensional. The realization that I was the one who was so wrong catapulted me into a paradigm shift that I have been unpacking ever since. My assumptions about myself, other people in my community, and my relationship with God completely shifted. One of the core issues I discovered was finding out that if a relationship isn't based on whether or not you're right, then it must mean that it's okay to be wrong.

The Truth

In the past, I felt that if I was wrong, I had failed. If had I failed, I was a failure. If I was a failure, I had no value and therefore no identity. And there the root issue is exposed. Performance. If I have to perform for identity, I have to perform for love. For there is nothing without love. If I have to perform to be loved, then can I ever actually be loved for *who* I am? The Lord showed me, in that simple question, that the maze ends right here—right at the gospel: "For this is how much God loved the world—He gave His one and only, unique Son as a gift. So now everyone who believes in him will never perish but experience everlasting life" (John 3:16 TPT).

Did you notice that there is no mention of "if we are good enough, if we accomplish enough, if we are kind enough, if we love enough, if we give enough, then God will love us enough to send His Son so we could be with Him forever"? That's why my relationships shifted. I began to see that, ultimately, my identity is summed up in one truth: that there is nothing I can do to earn God's love. Nothing. He loves me because I am me. He created me uniquely, wove me together intricately, and even loves my frailties! I have never known love that was totally accepting, nonjudgmental, void of all comparisons, and based upon nothing but *who* I am—except maybe from my wife.

This was all new for me. Realizing that He accepts me and He loves me like this was profoundly life altering. There are no words that can describe the revelation that in God's eyes, I was enough and that there was nothing I could do to alter His tenacious love for me. As a result, I also came to see that man's opinion of me had no correlation to who I am, to my value as a human being—to my core identity.

* * * * *

Have you found yourself in the same place, not recognizing God's tenacious love for you just as you are? If so, you don't have to remain there.

Father, please forgive me for every way that I believe lies that don't agree with the truth of who you reveal yourself to be in Scripture as fully loving, fully accepting, and fully receiving me as your child. I choose to receive your truth about me.

The Aftershock

I wish I had language that would adequately describe the impact this revelation had on me and my life. I wish there was a Richter scale for mind warps, because this had the spiritual magnitude of a 9.0 earthquake in my life. According to US Geological Survey documents, the damage a 9.0 event causes looks like this: "At or near total destruction—severe damage or collapse to all buildings. Heavy damage and shaking extends to distant locations. Permanent changes in ground topography."[2]

I had known for some time that my life's topography needed to change, but I had no power or ability to affect it. I desperately wanted my life to change. I was longing to be in some form of ministry and was absolutely confounded as to how to get out of this stagnant pit. Not a thing was changing, and there appeared to be nothing on the horizon that could bring any hope.

---

2   *Wikipedia*, s.v. "Richter Magnitude Scale," https://en.m.wikipedia.org/wiki/Richter_magnitude_scale.

After this profound epiphany, a major shift took place in my life. Metaphorically speaking, there was a collapse to all my buildings, heavy damage was done, the shaking extended to distant locations, and there were permanent changes in my topography. The truth had been opened up to me, my eyes were finally opened, and everything changed. My internal structures, my filtration system, and the belief system I had developed were all collapsing.

One of the many bizarre things about this was that it was *not* a correction. God tenderly wanted to show me myself. Father God wanted me to see *me*. It was like James 1:5 coming into my reality:

> And if anyone longs to be wise,
> ask God for wisdom and he will give it!
> He won't see your lack of wisdom as an
> opportunity to scold you over your failures
> but he will overwhelm your failures
> with his generous grace. (TPT)

> But if any of you lacks wisdom,
> let him ask of God, who gives to all men
> generously and without reproach,
> and it will be given to him. (NASB)

> If you need wisdom,
> ask our generous God,
> and he will give it to you.
> He will not rebuke you for asking.

Notice the theme evident in all these translations: He will not "scold you over your failures," He "will not rebuke you," and He will give "to all men generously and without reproach." Doing a word study on *reproach*, I found the meaning of the word revealed the heart of the Lord as He opened my eyes to who I was. *Without reproach* means without blame, without disgrace, without discredit, without criticizing, without finding fault, without reproof, without scorn or contempt. That was exactly how it felt. There was no reproof. This was a profound but tender revelation, from a kind and loving Father, that I sorely needed so my life could move forward. He answered the cry of my heart.

Story Weaving

A lot of current scientific research reveals that we are wired for story. I believe Jesus spoke in parables for that reason. As our creator, He knew all along what the latest science is now revealing. We understand stories. We create our own and weave them around our circumstances, whether they are based in reality or not. Sometimes I don't think we even know we are doing it. But that's what I did when I was stuck. I wove stories around what I was sure my life was going to look like when my "breakthrough" came and what this "breakthrough" would look like. Well, the Lord shattered all that. It was nothing like I could have ever imagined it.

My life changed from that moment on. My internal compass was spun. This was an astounding discovery—and alarming. I had to face a hard reality. People could actually see what I was trying to hide: my fear of failure, my fear of rejection, my fear of abandonment, my fear of not measuring up, fear of this or that or the other. I finally saw that my fears kept me unteachable, and that, simply put, God cannot use us if we are unteachable.

My worldview, or maybe I should say my "you view," was shaken. So much was exposed in that moment. I had no idea I was walking in such arrogance. I had no idea that I judged my entire community as untrustworthy. They were flawed, but I wasn't, because "me" and only "me" could I trust. How mind-blowing that I could not see any of this. It was like walking around thinking you look one way, then someone holds a mirror up to your face and you realize that you didn't even know what color eyes you had.

The Turning Point

My internal infrastructure crashed. It was a pivotal turning point as more awareness settled in. I became less sure of everything and everybody. I realized that before this epiphany, I measured the voices in my life by standards that I couldn't measure up to. Mark 12:31 unfolded in my heart: "You must love your neighbor in the same way you love yourself" (TPT). If I saw myself only as a failure, how could I possibly love myself? And if that was a correct assessment, if that was the lens that I saw myself through, then how could I really love those around me? But now, by the grace and goodness and kindness of God, I began to see things differently.

My attitude in the workplace changed. No longer was I quick to speak, quick to judge, and quick to assume I had all the answers. I would evaluate people carefully and much differently from before. I was quick to apologize and listened more than talked. I asked myself, "What if you're wrong here, Jeff?" instead of assuming I had all the answers.

My attitude at home changed too. Though I could give you my account of my home life after this revelation, I'll let my lovely Becky give you hers. The next section is in her words.

Becky's Account

I knew right away something major had happened in Jeff's life. The night of the experience, I noticed he was processing something and it was big. It was a heart change of some type.

He opened up to me and shared what the Lord was showing him. He then apologized to me for being so critical and shared the insights about Bethany and his boss and how wrong he had been there as well. He started showing more tenderness toward me and the kids, and became quick to apologize when necessary.

Jeff had to survive all his life. Rarely did he ever feel like anyone had his back. That belief created in him a lifestyle of defense where he felt he could only trust himself. Now I saw that changing. It was like something woke up inside of him—something he didn't even know needed to be awakened. His feelings and emotions were beginning to unlock, and they had been pretty tightly locked down before this.

He began showing me more respect. He would listen, and began weighing what I had to say as valuable and credible. He became much less defensive and didn't point a finger anymore. He was more caring and sensitive.

It was obvious that he could hear the Holy Spirit better and was more sensitive to Him. He spoke to the kids and me with more restraint and control. Instead of looking inward, he began to look outward more—and live more outwardly than inwardly. He started weighing thoughts, words, and actions before he would act or respond.

His life changed in an incredible way that day, and even to this day his life is still impacted by his revelation.

Getting Unstuck

My being stuck had everything to do with me ... being *stuck*. My own actions were causing my dilemma. I didn't know that I could not move forward until I understood this. All I knew was that I was doing everything I could possibly do. I was fasting and praying and binding and loosing, calling things down from heaven, etc., etc., etc. But what I didn't know was that I was walking around with an attitude of dishonor. And everyone could see it but me. I was like Pig-Pen from *Charlie Brown*, walking around in my own cloud of yuck.

The people God had placed in my life were trying to give me feedback on how they were experiencing me, but I wouldn't listen because I discounted them instead of thinking of them as being messengers from Him. I thought God would speak to me in His own personal, special, intimate way—like through the Word, a vision, a dream, or by sending a spiritual superhero or angelic visitation. But it came through my wife, little girl, and boss.

I also thought I understood Jesus' view on the marriage relationship. You know, wives should honor their husbands and husbands should lay down their lives for their wives as Christ gave His life for His church. I knew that at any given point I would step in front of a train for Becky. So I figured I had that one sewn up. Then the Lord gave me another look at 1 Peter 3:7:

> Husbands, you in turn must treat your
> wives with tenderness, viewing them as
> feminine partners who deserve to be hon-
> ored, for they are co-heirs with you of the
> "divine grace of life," *so that nothing will
> hinder your prayers.* (TPT)

In the same way, you husbands must give
honor to your wives. Treat your wife with
understanding as you live together. She
may be weaker than you are, but she is
your equal partner in God's gift of new life.
Treat her as you should *so your prayers will
not be hindered.*

In the same way, you husbands, live with
your wives in an understanding way [with
great gentleness and tact, and with an
intelligent regard for the marriage rela-
tionship], as with someone physically
weaker, since she is a woman. Show her
honor and respect as a fellow heir of the
grace of life, *so that your prayers will not be
hindered or ineffective.* (AMP)

Ouch! No wonder I was stuck. In every translation I found,
the message was inflexible. Honor your wives or your prayers will
be hindered. So because of the lack of respect I showed Becky by
thinking she was the one being too sensitive and being critical
and judgmental of me, my prayers were actually being hindered!
All along, I was the one holding the keys that would unlock my
breakthrough.

After this revelation, favor rolled in like a fog. My life did
begin to unlock. That impenetrable wall suddenly became full of
doors that started opening. Opportunities appeared. Things were
changing, and something new was being released. What I had
been looking for and kept yearning for finally came to pass.

* * * * *

Have you noticed aftershocks in your life after you've experienced a breakthrough? How have you handled those? Is there any "clean-up" that you need to address? Clean-up happens when we acknowledge our mistakes and ask for forgiveness.

Celebration, Not Competition

The favor of the Lord began to fall upon my life, and He eventually did open doors that led to opportunities for ministry. At last He was satisfying that longing in my heart. But along the way, He was teaching me more and more about kingdom principles. I want to share with you another lesson I learned, one that was so profound that it became the subject of the first sermon I ever preached.

All throughout my life, I have been privileged to have good close friends—friends that I can share my heart with, friends that I can laugh with, friends that challenge me, and friends that I can confide in. But as the Lord so often does, He put someone in my life who I was exceptionally close to. This friend and I were like spiritual blood brothers, cut from the same cloth. We had a unique relationship where I would hear something from the Lord that would be for him and he would hear something that was for me, and it caused us both to grow. I would encourage him, he would encourage me, and we would feed off each other as we walked through life. As we shared life's difficulties, challenges, joys, and victories, we couldn't help but grow closer in our friendship.

Sometime in the 1990s, we began to hear about a new prophetic movement in the church. We learned about the gift of prophecy and how God would use different people to bring a supernatural word of encouragement. One of the places where this was happening was in Kansas City. We kept hearing of Mike Bickle's church and all that was happening prophetically there. Miraculous stories were being told of how God would speak to people in mind-blowing ways. We were in awe of all the testimonies of how powerfully God was moving there.

My friend and I heard about a prophetic conference that was coming up in Kansas City, and we mentioned it to our pastor. He told us that he knew quite a few people out there and that he was planning to go, so he would be happy for us to go with him and he could introduce us to some of the folks that would be there. We were so excited. This was like a dream come true for me—I couldn't wait!

On the way to the conference, our pastor told us about a particular man who lived there—a man named Bob Lyons. He knew Bob and spoke highly of him: "This man is a sage, a genuine saint, and I really hope you guys get the opportunity to meet him."

When we got there, I could hardly contain myself. This was like Disney World for me! I had been waiting to be in this type of environment for so long. I walked in pure anticipation of what the Lord was going to do. I stood there, looking around, trying to take it all in. The atmosphere was electric.

Our pastor introduced us to different people. We were meeting some of the intercessors, several prophetic people, and some of the speakers, and the whole time I was giddy with expectation. I couldn't wait until I had my encounter with the Lord! I just knew, that I knew, that I knew that my time was coming and that it could happen at any moment.

The conference was sold out and very crowded. As we were getting registered, in the middle of all the activity, our pastor pointed out an older man walking our way. This man's countenance profoundly reflected Jesus. Our pastor introduced us. I couldn't believe it! It was Bob Lyons, the man he had told us about. This man walked in such a spirit of tenderness and joy. He laughed and cried, and cried and laughed. I couldn't tell if he was crying from laughing or laughing from crying. It was an honor and a joy to meet such a man.

The next morning, as the first session of the conference was about to start, we saw Bob Lyons passing by. We waved to him and said good morning. He made a bee-line toward us, pointed to my friend, and said, "Hey! I was thinking about you this morning, and I have a word for you."

I was so excited. I thought, *Oh my goodness! This is amazing!*

At this point, a lot of the people had cleared out, and it was just my friend and me with this prophet as he began to give my buddy an amazing word from the Lord. He prayed for my friend in a such profound way and said things like "Not only are you called, but you're *chosen*." Bob continued telling my friend that he would do all sorts of amazing things—that the Lord was going to do this and that for him, and it was all amazingly spot-on. This word went on and on and on. It was incredible. Knowing my friend and his life so well, I knew how accurate and impactful this word was for him.

I was in awe. I couldn't believe it was actually finally happening—the things that I had dreamed about, the things that I had heard about—and here it was happening, right now, right in front of my eyes. I was focused, intent on hearing everything so I could help my friend remember all that was said (we had no cell phones to make recordings then). And Bob's words just kept coming and coming. "The Lord has *divinely* called you," he continued. When Bob finally came to the end of this incredible word for my friend, he turned to me and said, "And *you* help him."

"Oh! All right. Okay, I will." I looked at my friend, and he was weeping and his head was obviously swirling with all that was just said to him.

This is so great! I can't wait for my turn. I thought. *Can't wait to hear what God says to me.*

Sobbing, my friend thanked him, and Bob started to walk away.

"Hey, Bob, what about me?" I said. "Would you pray for me?"

He turned around. "Sure." But it was as though the thought had never even crossed his mind. *That's weird*, I thought. He then proceeded to pray for me, saying about three words—and they were in tongues. And that was it. He just walked away.

I was shocked. *That's it? But doesn't God have anything to say to me? He doesn't have any more to say to me?* My thoughts spun as I just stood there.

Fighting dejection, my friend and I went in to the next session and found seats. Honestly, I was having a hard time. This whole thing tilted me. I was trying to keep myself in a good place but found it so difficult. I had been looking forward to receiving a word similar to what my friend just got. My hopes had been so high that God would say something to me, something about me, but now disappointment was setting in.

Worship began, and it was wonderful. I attempted to enter in, but had a hard time. Try as I might, I was struggling. My friend—now that was a different story. I looked over at him during worship, and he was undone before the Lord, pretty much just laid out before Him. He was justifiably ecstatic, weeping and worshiping his heart out. Every song had so much meaning for him. Everything was *living* to him in that moment. The world was bright, almost otherworldly to him. "Oh, my God … you are so great!" he cried out. "You are so good to me!"

I thought, *Yes, Lord. You are great. I know you are.* But my heart was not in it. My thoughts kept bombarding me. *Don't you care about me as much as you care about him? Has he become your favorite or something? What's wrong with me, Lord? Was there nothing else you could to say to me?* I couldn't figure out what was going on. Then I thought, *Whoa. What's the deal here? Jeff, why are you reacting like this?*

After the service that night, my friend and I talked about the word he got. He was walking on clouds. I was trying to walk right there with him, striving to share in his excitement. I told him how amazing it was, but, actually, I was having a hard time celebrating this incredible event in his life.

I woke up the next morning and this "thing" was still over me. I tried hard to brush it off, tried to shake it off. I listened as my friend processed all that had happened. He called his wife, and she shared his enthusiasm as well. I was really happy for my friend and was trying to be supportive of him, but as hard as I tried, I couldn't lose this "thing." My thoughts kept coming back to how I couldn't understand why God didn't say something to me. A subtle change began in my heart, and I realized that I might not be so happy for my friend after all.

It wasn't until the afternoon session when I had some time to myself during worship that I could finally ask the Lord, "Father, what's going on? What is wrong with me? Why can't I be happy for him? Why can't I celebrate him in this?"

The Lord spoke to me as clear as a bell, and He said, "The reason you're not happy for him and cannot celebrate him is because you're *competing* with him." Never was there a truer word spoken to me. It hit me in the center of my heart. The Lord had put His finger right on the issue.

"What? Oh, dear Lord. You're right. Oh, wow. I actually am *competing* with him." Bull's-eye. I knew right away that this was God's truth. Once again there was no condemnation. The Lord was so gentle. It actually gave me peace to know what I was wrestling with—and once again, I was wrestling with *me*.

I went to my friend and shared my revelation with him. I told him that ever since he received that incredible word, I had been struggling. I explained that all the things that were said in that prophecy were amazing but that it was the word that I had hoped and prayed that I would get. I shared that I could not celebrate him because I was stuck competing with him and was not aware of it, and I apologized for my behavior.

It is hard to describe what happened after the Lord opened my eyes to this whole revelation. He showed me it wasn't a new issue at all. I began to see stories in Scripture where competition reared its ugly head.

> Then the mother of James and John, the
> sons of Zebedee, came to Jesus with her
> sons. She knelt respectfully to ask a favor.
> "What is your request?" he asked. She

> replied, "In your Kingdom, please let my
> two sons sit in places of honor next to you,
> one on your right and one on your left."
> (Matthew 20:20–21)

Think about it: the most prominent places in the universe would be beside the Son of God, and this mother was asking that her two sons would monopolize those places forever. The other disciples were consumed with enough competition that it led to a big argument.

> When the other ten disciples heard what
> James and John had asked, they were
> indignant. But Jesus called them together
> and said, "You know that the rulers in
> this world lord it over their people, and
> officials flaunt their authority over those
> under them. But among you it will be
> different. Whoever wants to be a leader
> among you must be your servant, and
> whoever wants to be first among you
> must become your slave. For even the Son
> of Man came not to be served but to serve
> others and to give his life as a ransom for
> many." (Matthew 20:24–28)

Also look at what Paul told the Philippians: "It's true that some are preaching out of jealousy and rivalry. But others preach about Christ with pure motives" (Philippians 1:15).

The Lord taught me that competition is one of the roots of

division within the church. Now that I'm a pastor, I find that I have to really watch my heart, especially when I hear that the Lord is moving powerfully in another church, because if I'm not careful, I get stuck in comparing, which leads to competing instead of simply celebrating what God is doing.

It is so easy to get stuck, wrestling with this mind-set of competition, because our entire society is built upon it. Competition is the platform on which companies are built. Often it isn't enough to be the best; you have to take out your competitors as well. Companies compete with one another, departments compete with one another, and salespeople compete with one another. In order to get a promotion, you have to be better than the rest. When you graduate from college, your resume needs to be the best to get the job placement you need. From the beginning of your career to retirement, success revolves around competition. You have to be the best. That doesn't even touch our school systems and the competition our kids are taught from the beginning of their education. Unfortunately, everything in our society is based on winning … based on being the best … always having to fight to win.

Competition may be a huge factor in our society, but it does not belong in the church. The kingdom is not about competition. The kingdom is about celebration. It's thinking of others more than yourself. "Be free from pride-filled opinions, for they will only harm your cherished unity. Don't allow self-promotion to hide in your hearts, but in authentic humility put others first and view others as more important than yourselves" (Philippians 2:3 TPT).

The kingdom is all about supporting each other and lifting each other up, and, most importantly, *celebrating* each other. We should rejoice when something good happens to someone else.

The opposite of celebration is competition, and competition is actually rooted in jealousy. Scripture doesn't speak so well of jealousy either. Take a look:

> Surely resentment destroys the fool,
> and *jealousy* kills the simple. (Job 5:2)

> A peaceful heart leads to a healthy body;
> *jealousy* is like cancer in the bones.
> (Proverbs 14:30)

> Anger is cruel, and wrath is like a flood,
> but *jealousy* is even more dangerous.
> (Proverbs 27:4)

> "For I can see you are full of bitter *jealousy*
> and are held captive by sin." (Acts 8:23)

> Because we belong to the day, we must
> live decent lives for all to see. Don't participate in the darkness of wild parties
> and drunkenness, or in sexual promiscuity
> and immoral living, or in quarreling and
> *jealousy*. (Romans 13:13)

> For I am afraid that when I come I won't
> like what I find, and you won't like my
> response. I am afraid that I will find quarreling, *jealousy*, anger, selfishness, slander,

gossip, arrogance, and disorderly behavior.
(2 Corinthians 12:20)

When you follow the desires of your sinful
nature, the results are very clear: sexual
immorality, impurity, lustful pleasures,
idolatry, sorcery, hostility, quarreling, *jealousy*, outburst of anger, selfish ambition,
dissension, division, envy, drunkenness,
wild parties, and other sins like these. Let
me tell you again, as I have before, *that*
anyone living that sort of life will not inherit
the Kingdom of God. (Galatians 5:19–21)

When we allow competition to affect us, jealousy *will* have a place in our hearts. You can plainly see how the Lord lumps jealousy in with some serious sins and outlines the dangers of walking in that spirit. I believe it is a grossly underestimated offense that carries with it grave spiritual dangers. We must learn to lay our lives down for others. We also must learn that it is okay for someone else to get the trophy. I believe that as we serve others and practice celebrating those the Lord has placed in our lives, their accomplishments, their blessings, and their giftings, our hearts will be kept pure from the bitterness and resentment that accompanies jealously.

You've probably heard it said that the kingdom of heaven is like upside-down thinking. That couldn't be truer. The greatest is the least, and the least is the greatest. The first is the last, and the last is the first. Jesus, the Exalted Son of Almighty God, the One at whose name all knees will bow, lowered Himself to be a servant to all mankind, showing us what kingdom living looks like. Let's not be hesitant in embracing His example.

Though the Lord may reveal profound things to us, if we don't comprehend that it is *His* opinion of us that matters and it is what *He* says and thinks and feels about us that we base our self-worth upon, then we will continue harboring beliefs that are detrimental to our lives and our destinies.

* * * * *

Though my belief system was being adjusted, at this point in my life, I found myself believing …

- He will bless others, but He won't bless me.
- I must have done something to deserve being left out.
- He must love others more than me.

Father, forgive me for any way that I have fallen back to old belief systems that don't line up with your truth. Please forgive me for any jealousy or envy that I have harbored toward others and forgive me for believing the lie that your blessings are limited.

14

Avoiding Self-Promotion

The Lord showed me something else that was a driving lie at the core of competition. He revealed that I was believing that there was only one spot of favor and God was deciding who was going to get it. Frankly, it felt like He gave that last spot of favor to my friend. It might sound silly when you look at it that way, but I think this might be a lie that many Christians stumble over and don't even realize it. I was certainly blindsided by it. I was walking as if God rations out places in the kingdom, and there were only a few left and the last one went to my friend. Nothing could be further from the truth! *Everyone* has a place in His kingdom!

When God opened my eyes to this and I determined to lay down competition, He also showed me there was a little more to it than that—I had to also lay down self-promotion. I didn't realize that in competing with my friend, I had a hidden motive of self-promotion at work. As the Lord revealed this to me, He reminded me of something that I knew in my head but had not been activated in my heart.

According to His Word, the only way promotion actually comes to us is from Him. More dominoes began to fall. I was "hit between the lies"—and I crumbled. This was another paradigm buster. I didn't realize that I had been wrestling with self-promotion. But I clearly was—it was like this "thing" had a pulse and was trying to drive me—and I had no idea! Again, I couldn't move forward in my life.

The Lord opened up His Word and showed me His heart regarding promotion in Isaiah 42: "Look at my servant, whom I strengthen. He is my chosen one, who pleases me. I have put my Spirit upon him. He will bring about justice in the nations. He will not shout or raise his voice in public. He will not crush the weakest reed or put out a flickering candle" (vv. 1–3).

Wow. This is the what the God of the universe is saying: "Hey, everyone! Look over here—look at this! Do you see this person? This is the one that I'm endorsing. This is the one I choose to promote—the one who doesn't raise his voice in the street. In other words, the one who won't draw attention to himself. Or another way of saying it is that he won't promote himself. The one I promote will also care about weak people and treat them gently and tenderly—a bruised reed he will not break, or put out a flickering candle."

The one the Lord chooses to promote will not promote himself. That's what the Lord was talking about. And competition is actually about promoting yourself.

Take a look at what else the Word of the Lord says about promotion:

This I know: the favor that brings promotion and power doesn't come from anywhere on earth, for no one exalts a person but God, the true judge of all. He alone determines where favor rests. He anoints one for greatness and brings another down to his knees. (Psalm 75:6–7 TPT)

If you bow low in God's awesome presence, he will eventually exalt you as you leave the timing in his hands.
(1 Peter 5:6 TPT)

The Pattern of Humility

Look at the pattern here. God *alone* is the one who promotes! He lifts up the lowly. Furthermore, if you bow in His presence, He will exalt you—if you leave the timing in His hands. If you can embrace humility and celebrate others who have been promoted or encouraged in the Lord, then get ready. His favor will be coming to *you*. Just remember, He is God. Leave the timing and the methods in His hands.

Unfortunately, we tend to think that if we don't promote ourselves, we will never get promoted. And if we don't promote ourselves, how will others know who we are? How can we measure our worth if it isn't through promotion or competition or winning or being the first or being the best in man's eyes? Remember, what you have to fight to get, you have to fight to keep.

"Unless the Lord builds a house, the work of the builders is wasted" (Psalm 127:1). If we try to build our own "house"—our own reputations, our own image—and don't realize that our promotion has to come from the Lord, our work is *wasted*. We cannot confuse promotion with validation or worth. Our worth must be summed up in the realization that God tenderly and passionately loves us—just like we are right in this moment, just where we are right now.

We need to understand that He loves us so much that it actually *pleased* our heavenly Father to bruise the only, tenderly loved Son that He had so that our redemption would be made possible. And He did this for one reason: that we could be *His*, be co-heirs with His Son forever. "But it was the Lord's good plan to bruise him and fill him with grief. However, when his soul has been made an offering for sin, then he shall have a multitude of children, many heirs" (Isaiah 53:10 TLB).

A Modern-Day Example

One of the most powerful testimonies I've seen regarding self-promotion is from my friend Surprise Sithole, who lives in Mozambique. He is one of my dearest friends and the most supernatural person I have ever met. Miracles just seem to follow him: the blind see, the deaf hear, and even then dead are raised.

Once when he was at our church, I witnessed God's supernatural hand move right in front of me. A young child had a heart disorder that would require open heart surgery to repair, and the parents asked him to pray for their baby. He held the little one during worship and sang over her. After worship ended, he gave the child back to her parents and said that she was healed and that she would be fine. When the parents took the baby back to the doctor, he could find nothing wrong with her!

Years ago, a prominent Christian magazine heard about

Surprise—specifically about a little girl being raised from the dead when he prayed for her. They flew their team to Africa to get the story firsthand from him and followed him around for several days, looking for the right opportunity to interview him. But to their astonishment, when they finally had a chance to get his story firsthand, he ignored them. He would not tell them about it.

My pastor at the time was there and watched all this happen. He asked Surprise why he was shunning these reporters. "Why won't you tell them about the little girl who was raised from the dead?"

I will never forget his answer. It was stunning. Surprise said, "I have found that when *I* talk about me, God's anointing on my life goes down. But when *God* talks about me, His anointing on my life goes up. So I prefer to have God talk about me instead of me." What a profound perspective!

It is an act of God's goodness that He wants us to get this message. When we begin to understand His nature, to understand how much He treasures us and wants good things for us, we start to trust that He really does love us and has no plans to leave us out. As a matter of fact, He wants us to leave our place of striving for our own promotion and give the responsibility to Him. He can be trusted with it! If we can do that, He will lead us to a place of rest where we are no longer the one striving for our own validation. We can rest in Him, knowing He loves us. He has us, He is faithful, and He is reliable.

Bringing It Home

We have to stop believing that we are being left out when we see something good happen to someone else. We have to get the message that if He's doing something good for one of His kids, He's going to do it for another: "If you, imperfect as you are, know how to lovingly take care of your children and give them what's best, how much more ready is your heavenly Father to give wonderful gifts to those who ask him?" (Matthew 7:11 TPT).

If we can get this revelation and get it deep into the core of who we are, it will be a tectonic shift in our foundation that will alter the rest of our life. If we can get this, we can enter His rest. This awareness creates rest. All competition and all self-promotion is done from a place of unrest, from a place of striving.

> But if you are bitterly jealous and there is
> selfish ambition in your heart, don't cover
> up the truth with boasting and lying. For
> jealously and selfishness are not God's
> kind of wisdom. Such things are earthly,
> unspiritual, and demonic. For wherever
> there is jealously and selfish ambition,
> there you will find disorder and evil of
> every kind. (James 3:14–16)

But when we understand the nature of our Father, we can stop our striving and let Him take over. He is trying to get us to that "Ahhhh …" moment of real rest, of really letting go. That's why Jesus could sleep in a boat in the middle of a storm so fierce that it terrified seasoned fishermen. He was able to let Himself rest in His Father's care because He knew His Father had Him. It wasn't complicated. He knew His Father's nature because He knew His Father's love. That's the kind of rest He is offering us.

* * * * *

The Lord is my best friend and my shepherd. I always have more than enough. He offers a resting place for me in His luxurious love. His tracks take me to an oasis of peace, the quiet brook of bliss. That's where He restores and revives my life. He opens before me pathways to God's pleasure and leads me along in His footsteps of righteousness so that I can bring honor to His name. Lord, even when your path takes me through the valley of deepest darkness, fear will never conquer me, for you already have! You remain close to me and lead me through it all the way. Your authority is my strength and my peace. The comfort of your love takes away my fear. I'll never be lonely, for you are near. You become my delicious feast even when my enemies dare to fight. You anoint me with the fragrance of your Holy Spirit; you give me all I can drink of you until my heart overflows. So why should I fear the future? For your goodness and love pursue me all the days of my life. Then afterward, when my life is through, I'll return to your glorious presence to be forever with you! (Psalm 23 TPT)

Two Rights Don't Make a Wrong

A decade or so after this colossal revelation in my life, the Lord challenged me in an area that I found pretty tough. This involved my daughter, Bethany. Understand that I am so proud of my kids. She and her brother have hearts that seek after God, and both are intent on hearing His voice. I am incredibly grateful that the Lord gave us Bethany and Joel. There are no words that can describe the depth of love I have for them. The integrity and faithfulness they walk in is so impressive. I can truly say that my son and daughter delight my heart. That is the reason that what I am about to share with you was not only spiritually challenging to me but emotionally challenging as well.

At the beginning of the summer leading up to Bethany's junior year of high school, she had a revelation from the Lord. She said the Lord told her she was to graduate early that year by working hard and studying at home instead of continuing at the high school. Then she said the Lord wanted her to go to another country and be a part of a well-known ministry. As I said earlier, I know my daughter has incredible ears to hear the voice of the Lord. Because I trusted that she was hearing His voice on this, I did not want to discourage her. I was going to allow her room to dream and bask in this exciting place of hope and expectation.

But a strange thing happened. The more that time passed, the more uneasy I felt. No matter what I did, I couldn't shake it. I didn't have peace about this anymore. And I didn't know why. I kept praying, "Lord, she's hearing from you. I don't doubt that. So why don't I have peace about this?" Not wanting to force anything or discourage her, I continued to pray and seek the Lord on this. Maybe I was missing something.

That summer, things got tough. Her excitement escalated. She started telling her friends that she wasn't coming back to school because she was going to homeschool, graduate early, and leave the country to be a part of this ministry. Becky also shared our daughter's enthusiasm: "This is awesome! This is going to happen for her, and she's going to love it!" But I never could come to a place of peace about it, and I didn't know why. At times I thought, *Am I even saved?* Becky and Bethany were sure that the Lord was leading in this and that I would eventually catch up to their revelation.

Finally, I felt I had to step in. I told Bethany that I didn't have peace about this decision. My paddle in the pond had a pretty severe ripple effect. Bethany was absolutely convinced that God was going to speak to me and I would change my mind. Becky thought I was holding our daughter back. "Why aren't you supporting her in this?" she would ask.

The uncomfortable division between us brought me to a place of desperate introspection. I sought the Lord fervently:

"Lord, what's wrong here? What's wrong with me? Why don't I have peace about this? What's going on that there is such a separation, such discord around this thing?" But try as I might, I could not find any peace in her going through with this.

I kept referring back to the passage, "Let the peace that comes from Christ rule in your hearts" (Colossians 3:15). Then I gave Bethany to the Lord's care and prayed, "Just confirm it to me, Lord. I don't understand this, but you know that I don't have peace about it. I'm pretty desperate for your direction, because I have to know what to do here."

The more I prayed, the less peace I had in her going. I knew the Holy Spirit led through peace, and I was trying my best to follow His lead. I was perplexed because every time I would sit before the Lord regarding this, I had less and less peace regarding Bethany's plan.

The way I'm naturally wired is to have peace in my relationships. I did not have peace. All the voters in my home were on one side of this decision and I was alone on the other. This was a very hard place for me. However, I was certain that God was speaking to me about this situation through my uneasiness. My being all alone in this carried some benefit. As I rode solo, I pressed in closer to the Lord. I knew this decision was monumental in my daughter's life, and I felt every bit of that pressure. The more time I spent before the Father, the more I became confident I was hearing Him correctly. I knew I had to stick to my decision and follow my heart's peace in this.

The week before school started, things got into the red zone in our house. I asked Bethany if she had registered for school, and she had not. When I told her that it was time to do that, she was undone.

"Dad, I've heard from God that I'm supposed to go!" she pleaded. "I know I am!"

"Honey, I'm sorry, but I just don't have peace about this," I replied. "I just don't."

So on the day of registration, things were a bit icy. She wouldn't even look at me as we walked into the school. I could see she was holding back a dam of tears that she didn't want to release at school.

As we were walking down the hall for her to register for a class, a teacher saw her and cried out, "Bethany! You're back! We're so glad to see you here!"

I thought, *Wow, she has a lot of favor here! And thank you, God.*

Registration was on Friday, and school started that next Monday. All weekend Bethany still remained convinced that God was going to speak to me and change my mind before school started. Unfortunately, I got no other word from the Lord that would change the way I felt in my heart, no matter how difficult it was for me to stand my ground. Being a father, I hate to disappoint my kids, but I knew I had to follow the peace in my heart, and there was nothing that had happened that changed that lack of peace.

We lived across the street from the school, so when Monday arrived, we could hear the hustle and bustle of the cars and buses go by. Bethany was sitting on the couch with her head down. She started to weep.

Fighting tears myself, I said, "Bethany, we need to get ready to go. We have to leave soon."

"But, Dad, God told me! I don't understand why you're doing this. Don't you think I heard from the Lord?"

My heart was in a vice—truly stuck between a rock and hard place. Still, I knew what the Lord had told me to do. Then the Lord reminded me of a situation in Scripture, in the life of Jesus when He was young.

Every year Jesus' parents went to Jerusalem for the Passover festival. When Jesus was twelve years old, they attended the festival as usual. After the celebration was over, they started home to Nazareth, but Jesus stayed behind in Jerusalem. His parents didn't miss him at first, because they assumed he was among the other travelers. But when he didn't show up that evening, they started looking for him among their relatives and friends. When they couldn't find him, they went back to Jerusalem to search for him there. Three days later they finally discovered him in the Temple, sitting among the religious teachers, listening to them and asking questions. All who heard him were amazed at his understanding and his answers.

His parents didn't know what to think. "Son," his mother said to him, "why have you done this to us? Your father and I have been frantic, searching for you everywhere."

"But why did you need to search?" he

asked. "Didn't you know that I must be in
my Father's house?" But they didn't understand what he meant.
Then he returned to Nazareth with them
and was obedient to them. And his
mother stored all these things in her heart.
Jesus grew in wisdom and in stature and
in favor with God and all the people. (Luke
2:41–52)

As I thought about this unique story in Jesus' life, the Lord opened up some things for me. First of all, can you imagine the panic in Mary and Joseph? I wonder if they ever looked at each other and said, "What have we done? We've lost Him. The Savior of the world! How could this have happened? We were given one job."

I remember when I was four years old, I loved playing games. Hide and Seek was one of my favorites. So I came up with the bright idea of hiding from my parents. I found a very clever hiding place—right in their closet. I was fairly certain they would never find me there. And I was right. I heard them calling, and at first I thought it was so funny. I whisper-giggled at how clever I was. Then I realized that as they called me—over and over again—their voices started getting a little more excited. After more time passed, they started sounding concerned. Then they sounded panicked. Finally, I came out and showed myself. Well, they may have been relieved to see me, but let's just say that things didn't go exactly as I thought they would. Actually, they didn't go well for me at all. I never tried that again!

Today, I get why it didn't go so well for me. They were worried sick. As a parent, I would have been as well. When Mary and

Joseph couldn't find Jesus, they were justifiably frantic. Having searched everywhere—the caravan, their friends and family, the back of the donkey—finally they headed back to Jerusalem. How worried they must have been! He had been missing for days. Then they finally found Him in the temple, hanging out with the older guys, listening to their teachings, asking them questions, and holding His own in the conversations.

You can understand why Mary said, "Son, why have you done this to us? We have been frantically looking for you everywhere!" Then Jesus responded, "But why were you looking everywhere for me? Wouldn't you have known that I would be about my Father's business?"

"But they didn't understand what He meant," we are told. Right there—right at that moment—I personally believe all of heaven stood at attention and was waiting to see what Jesus would do next. You see, Jesus was right. He had heard from His Father and was taking care of His business. I think we underestimate this moment in history. Sometimes, we can become so familiar with a story that we lose the dimensional impact it carries. We don't realize that our salvation actually rests upon what this twelve-year-old boy would do next.

Let's take a second and look at what the boy Jesus *did not* do and what He *did not* say. Notice that He *did not* say, "Mom, do you not see what you are about to do here? Do you not remember who I am?" He also *did not* say, "Do you not remember that time when Gabriel came walking into your room and said, 'Hello, highly favored woman of God,' and you said, 'Wow, that's an unusual greeting'? Then he tells you all about *me*? Well, this is *me*, I'm the One that he was talking about. I'm the One that was sent here! And I'm doing what my Father told me to do. So, Mom, can you not see that you guys are interfering and that you're about to stop a movement of God here?" He also *did not* say, "I must obey God rather than man." And He *did not* add, "But the Lord told me to."

He did *not* do or say any of that even though He had every right to do so. I think we need to give attention to the things He did *not* say or do because they are imperative here. That is what we need to pay attention to. He did not defend Himself. He did not push back at all. But what He did do next reveals the economy of heaven. The Word says this: "And He went down with them and came to Nazareth, and He continued in *subjection* to them" (Luke 2:51 NASB). What we see demonstrated right here is that, in the economy of heaven, it is more valuable to come under authority than it is to be right.

The story continues with some translations saying "Then" and some saying "And," but both words connect the previous statement with the next, which is, "And Jesus kept increasing in wisdom and stature and *favor with God* and man." So the question is, how can the Son of God *grow* in favor with Father God? That doesn't make sense. But He did. The fact that these two events *are connected*, that they are tied together, shows that Jesus' action of submission actually caused the favor of His Father to come to Him. Now, if Jesus, the Son of God, needed to grow in favor with God and man, how much more do I?

When the Lord dropped this into my spirit, I was at a crisis point. I was desperate to be able to understand what was happening with my family. Suddenly, I saw that we are all capable and are all going to hear from God sometime in our lives. Often, those who are in authority over us, just like Mary, will not understand it. At that very point in our life, all of heaven is looking to see what we will do next. If we hold on to our need to be right, we are going to push our case and argue our point and miss the favor the Lord has waiting for us.

We need to realize that this is not about being right or wrong. I knew that there was no one in the world who could convince Bethany that she did not hear from the Lord. Actually, you couldn't convince me of that either. That's what made this so tough. God showed me through this revelation that, in the economy of heaven, being right is not the most important thing—coming under authority and being in submission is. Once again, the Word says that Mary did not understand. We need to realize when those in authority do not understand us, all of heaven is watching to see our response.

I realized that a value statement of heaven was being revealed to me through this story in Scripture and that it was exactly what Bethany was facing. So I shared the story with her. "Honey, I do believe with all my heart that you heard from the Lord," I told her. "Jesus also heard from God when He was twelve years old and stayed behind in the temple. His mother asked Him why He had caused them to be so worried. Bethany, right here in Scripture, when Jesus answered them, it plainly says that Mary and Joseph didn't understand what Jesus was saying. Was Jesus wrong?"

"No," she answered.

"Was Mary wrong?" I continued.

"No."

"Did Jesus ever sin?'

"No."

"Actually, neither of them were wrong. In fact, both of them had different perspectives and both of them were right," I went on. "But because Jesus was under the God-given authority of

His parents, He submitted to them. He had been 'right.' Yet, they had been 'right.' Even so, Jesus submitted to their 'right.' You see, because God so values authority, even Jesus had to come under the authority of His earthly parents. When He did this, He was also submitting to His heavenly Father. This was part of His preparation for His public ministry in His Father's perfect timing and His Father's perfect way. I sincerely believe it will be the same for you."

I finished, "I really do believe that you heard from the Lord, Bethany. And I also believe that God did not give me a peace about it. I know this has been difficult, but you need to know that this experience, and what God is showing you through it, is actually vital to your spiritual growth and very important in your relationship with Him."

Bethany went to school that year and it turned out to be the best school year of her life. In case you might be thinking that's an easy thing for me to say, I have asked Bethany to give her account so you can judge for yourself. The next section is in her words.

Bethany's Story

The summer before my junior year in high school, I heard the Lord tell me that I was to finish my studies early by working hard at home and then go to a specific worship school that happened to be in another country. I was so excited. My mom was all for it and was thrilled for me as well. However, my dad was a bit hesitant.

I was determined though. I had heard from the Lord, so I knew He was going to work it all out. I went through the summer holding tightly to that belief. However, the closer we got to summer's end, the more my dad wasn't budging. And it wasn't because he just wanted to be mean. I could tell that he didn't have a peace like Mom and I had. That being said, I firmly believed that the Lord could work a "suddenly" here and change my dad's heart and give him the peace he wanted to have to be able to bless me in this. I prayed all summer that the Lord would do something like send an angel to appear to him to show him God's heart in this.

When the day came to register for classes, I was certain God would have given Dad a dream or a vision or something during the night that would change his mind. But He didn't. When Dad got up that morning and told me it was time to go register, I was devastated. I wept and wept but not out of manipulation. I knew Dad couldn't be manipulated anyway. My heart was just broken. I felt that Dad was robbing me of my dream and it was so unfair. I was incredibly angry with him and terribly confused. I knew that I had heard the Lord.

On the way to register, the car ride was a bit tense. I remember pressing my entire body tightly against the door to create as much space as humanly possible between my dad and me. I was working hard to get my point across.

The Monday that school started, Dad came to me and read in Luke about Jesus being at the temple and his parents being worried about Him. He asked me who was the one who was wrong—Jesus or His parents? I told him neither. Then he continued to explain about the lesson on authority in that passage.

Well, by that time I was pretty certain I was not going to be studying at home, so I poured out my heart to the Lord. I told Him that even though I didn't understand all this, if He wanted me back in school, I needed a confirmation and a reason. It didn't take long for that to happen. Within the first week, one of my friends confided to me that she was pregnant. That's when all the pieces began to come together for me, and at that point, I knew that it was God's will for me to be right where I was. I was able to come alongside her during the most incredibly intense time of her life.

From there, it just kept getting better. The friendships the Lord gave me that year just blew my mind. I love people, and my friends are so important to me. I had good friends in my life up to that point, but this year, my friendships were those I had only dreamed of. I joined a campus ministry, and for the first time in a public-school setting, I was able to do life with school friends who really loved the Lord in such a deep way. They shared my hunger for going deeper in relationship in the Lord. We were able to have such rich experiences together, and we grew closer to Jesus and each other because of that. We were even able to study the Word, bring in guest speakers, bring in worship leaders, and pray for each other and for God to move in our school. It was incredible! It was the most amazing school year I had ever experienced.

I came out of this agonizing adventure with a deep awareness of the power of submission. I finally understood that, by submitting to my parents, I was ultimately submitting to the Lord. It also changed my relationship with my dad in an amazing way. I found myself wanting to run everything by him after that whole experience.

Both my junior year and my senior year were incredible. They were actually the best years of my high school experience. As a matter of fact, those two years were so good that it redefined my perspective on school. I had struggled a bit in previous years with grades and came away from those years with the belief that I just wasn't a very good student or capable of making good grades. However, in my senior year, I made straight A's!

Eventually, after graduation, I did go to a worship school.

I saw again and again that it was God's perfect timing. As I look back, I can see how I was directed and protected from complications that would have affected my life. Some of these complications may have even kept me from going to college. Simply put, I knew how well the years went after that event, and I knew it was a direct result of honoring Dad's voice.

I never understood fully the value of coming under authority. I knew it was a "requirement," but I never knew the blessings it could bring to someone's life. I cannot even begin to tell you all the favor that started falling on me from that time that I gave in and listened to Dad. It was genuinely a time when my life took a definite turn in all the right ways. I could tell that I was better prepared for the worship school when I finally went. I knew that the timing was perfect. I could hear the Lord better, and I know I gained discernment. I can truly say that this incident shifted my life.

I have always loved my dad, but I now began seeing him in a different light. My relationship with him started going much deeper. I trusted him more, and because of that, we grew closer. I knew that this was as hard for him as it was for me, and I knew that his heart for me was only for my good, but at the time, that didn't really matter. Now it does.

When I was asked why God would tell me yes and my dad no, I thought about it and felt that it was just a test of *my* heart. This was simply about me answering the question, "Will you honor and trust me by coming under the authorities I have put in your life?" I can say with all assurance that this event, this lesson, redefined my life.

* * * * *

Are there authorities in your life that you have dishonored, rejected, or rebelled against? Ask the Lord if He has a perspective about them that you haven't seen before. Ask the Lord what He would like for you to do in order to make things right.

Lord, I confess that you've put authorities in my life for a purpose, and even if they're not perfect, I choose to trust you and your plan.

16

Ring of Power

One of my favorite stories is J.R.R. Tolkien's *Lord of the Rings* series. It is a brilliant allegory about a special ring that possessed unlimited power. However, there was a danger and an adverse effect on the person who wore the ring. Anything lying dormant in the heart of the wearer, any hidden motives or secret ambitions, would come out and possess the wearer. If they had a hidden quest for power, they would become the most powerful one over all of creation. If the person was devious, evil would be the result. If they were vain, the whole world would be mesmerized by them and fall on their faces in adoration.

This ring had been hidden for centuries, but now it had resurfaced, and something had to be done with it. A lowly little hobbit, Frodo, offered to take the ring to the faraway place where it could be destroyed. He was one of the smallest creatures, not very strong and the most unlikely one to go on such a dangerous adventure. Yet he was humble, courageous, and, though insignificant by all appearances, in his heart he was content and harbored no guile. He was the only one who could carry the ring because he had the heart of a humble child.

I think Tolkien created an incredible allegory of what can happen in our own hearts when our identity is attached to our successes. A friend of mine was telling me of a situation at his company that had him perplexed. Several months earlier, a leadership position opened up at his company. His company was Christian based, so they used an intense vetting process that they felt was necessary before they brought anyone on board, especially as a supervisor.

My friend knew of someone with an outstanding reputation who was looking for a job and would be a perfect fit to fill the position. This person's references were incredible. Everyone my friend talked to had observed the same things about this guy. He was a person of strong character; was kind, respectful, and humble; had a healthy marriage and family life; and possessed all the credentials that would be needed for the job. The man seemed a perfect fit, so my friend hired him.

Things started out well, but within a few months, people began to notice an overall change in the attitude of this man. His demeanor changed from being approachable, peaceful, kind, and humble to being more condescending and stern. Other employees in the office found ways to work around this guy and avoid him. At times, everyone would go out for lunch. My friend told me this man treated the servers with distain. He would look down his nose through his glasses at the menu and not even look at the server when he ordered. He would even shoo him away with a dismissive wave of his hand. He acted like he was living on a social strata above all others.

Things went from bad to worse. The other employees began making complaints. The man's haughtiness and conceit affected the atmosphere of the office. He talked down to his coworkers, especially females. He began to walk in privilege around the office, and eventually questions came up that couldn't be answered regarding funds and supplies. My friend was more and more baffled at the change in this man. What happened? He went from Dr. Jekyll to Mr. Hyde and no one saw it coming.

Eventually, my friend had no choice but to let the man go. He was relieved when the guy was finally gone, but he was grieved at how this man changed. We talked about how someone with such high character and moral convictions, someone who was kind and caring, someone who by all appearances walked in humility and honored God, could change so radically. Was it the ring of power?

In the fourth chapter in the book of Daniel, the Lord showed me something in the life of King Nebuchadnezzar that is relevant to this. The story begins with the king blessing his people and basking in God's blessing:

> King Nebuchadnezzar sent this message
> to the people of every race, and nation
> and language throughout the world:
> "Peace and prosperity to you! I want
> you all to know about the miraculous
> signs and wonders the Most High God
> has performed for me. How great are
> His signs, how powerful His wonders!
> His kingdom will last forever, His rule
> through all generations.

"I, Nebuchadnezzar, was living in my
palace in comfort and prosperity. But one
night I had a dream that frightened me; I
saw visions that terrified me as I lay in my
bed. So I issued an order calling in all the
wise men of Babylon, so they could tell
me what my dream meant. When all the
magicians, enchanters, astrologers, and
fortune-tellers came in, I told them the
dream, but they could not tell me what it
meant. At last, Daniel came in before me,
and I told him the dream." (Daniel 4:1–8)

The king told Daniel he had a nightmare that really shook
him up and then told Daniel the dream:

"These were the visions of my head while
on my bed: I was looking, and behold,
a tree in the midst of the earth, and its
height was great. The tree grew and
became strong; its height reached to the
heavens, and it could be seen to the ends
of all the earth. Its leaves were lovely, its
fruit abundant, and in it was food for all.
The beasts of the field found shade under
it, the birds of the heavens dwelt in its
branches, and all flesh was fed from it.
"I saw in the visions of my head while on
my bed, and there was a watcher, a holy
one, coming down from heaven. He cried

aloud and said thus: 'Chop down the tree
and cut off its branches, strip off its leaves
and scatter its fruit. Let the beasts get
out from under it, and the birds from its
branches. Nevertheless leave the stump
and roots in the earth, bound with a band
of iron and bronze, in the tender grass
of the field. Let it be wet with the dew of
heaven, and let him graze with the beasts
on the grass of the earth. Let his heart be
changed from that of a man, let him be
given the heart of a beast, and let seven
times pass over him. This decision is by the
decree of the watchers, and the sentence
by the word of the holy ones, in order that
the living may know that the Most High
rules in the kingdom of men, gives it to
whomever He will, and sets over it the
lowest of men.'" (Daniel 4:10–17 NKJV)

When Daniel heard the details of the dream, he was scared
for the king. The king noticed and told him not to be afraid. But
Daniel, knowing what the dream meant, told the king that he sincerely wished that the dream was meant for the king's enemies
and not for the king himself. He gives the king the Lord's inter-
pretation:

"This is what the dream means, your Maj-
esty, and what the Most High has declared
will happen to my lord the king. You will

> be driven from human society, and you
> will live in the fields with the wild animals.
> You will eat grass like a cow, and you will
> be drenched with the dew of heaven.
> Seven periods of time will pass while you
> live this way, until you learn that the Most
> High rules over the kingdoms of the world
> and gives them to anyone He chooses.
> But the stump and roots of the tree were
> left in the ground. This means that you will
> receive your kingdom back again when
> you have learned that heaven rules.
> "King Nebuchadnezzar, please accept
> my advice. Stop sinning and do what is
> right. Break from your wicked past and be
> merciful to the poor. Perhaps then you will
> continue to prosper." (Daniel 4:24–27)

Once again, the Lord's messenger was ignored. The king didn't take that somber warning seriously or listen to the messenger the Lord sent to him. Daniel pleaded for Nebuchadnezzar to heed the warning God had sent to him, but the king did not heed his advice.

> "But all these things did happen to King
> Nebuchadnezzar. Twelve months later he
> was walking on the flat roof of the royal
> palace in Babylon. As he looked out across
> the city, he said, 'Look at this great city of
> Babylon! By my own mighty power, I have

built this beautiful city as my royal resi-
dence to display my majestic splendor.'
"While these words were in his mouth, a
voice called down from heaven, 'O King
Nebuchadnezzar, this message is for you!
You are no longer ruler of this kingdom.
You will be driven from human society.
You will live in the fields with the wild
animals, and you will eat grass like a cow.
Seven periods of time will pass while you
live this way, until you learn that the Most
High rules over the kingdoms of the world
and gives them to anyone He chooses.'
"That same hour the judgment was
fulfilled, and Nebuchadnezzar was driven
from human society. He ate grass like a
cow, and he was drenched with the dew of
heaven. He lived this way until his hair was
as long as eagles' feathers and his nails
were like birds' claws." (Daniel 4:28–33)

The Watchers

This story opens with heavenly watchers looking over the
earth. It appears that this heavenly council had met and was looking over the books. It was brought to their attention that Nebuchadnezzar had been given great authority, power, and domin-
ion, yet he was found wanting. He had no humility. They decided
they needed to fix this, so they came up with a plan and decided
they would give him a heads-up. Yet this was such an important

message that they came to him and made this announcement face-to-face in a dream. They told him that they wanted him to understand something: "The Most High is sovereign over all kingdoms on earth and gives them to anyone He wishes and sets them over the *lowliest of people*." (Daniel 4:17 NIV).

They basically said, "We have looked at your life and found you wanting. According to His government, you have more authority than you have humility. We have seen the scales of your life, and they are tipped in the wrong direction. You see, the ones who the Most High appoints must have a necessary amount of humility in their life, and it is quite clear that you don't. Therefore, in order for you to continue to rule, you have to abide by His kingdom principles, and one of His kingdom principles is that a successful kingdom ruler must possess humility. When you are given a massive amount of authority, you need a massive amount of humility to balance it. In other words, how did you slip through? We intend to help you balance the scales of your life so you can continue to rule. You have too much pride to have this much authority. The scales have to be balanced. The only way for you to continue to rule is for you to have a measure of humility inserted into your life."

Though this interaction from the watchers seems severe, it is not so much a punishment as it is a favor. Actually, this is God's favor coming upon the king. You see, in His kingdom, according to His ways, authority and humility must go hand in hand. Nebuchadnezzar had too much authority and not enough humility. Therefore, they chose to balance the scales and bring a certain amount of humility instead of removing him. This was a vote in his favor. They could have killed him; instead, they allowed him to live and rule—but only after he had learned humility.

Before disaster the heart of a man is
haughty and filled with self-importance,
but humility comes before honor.
(Proverbs 18:12 AMP)

No Longer Wanting

Fortunately for the king, his story didn't end there. Just as the Word of the Lord said, after seven years passed, things changed for him. I love what the Lord does in this part of the story:

"After this time had passed, I, Nebuchadnezzar, looked up to heaven. My sanity
returned, and I praised and worshiped the
Most High and honored the one who lives
forever.

"His rule is everlasting, and his kingdom
is eternal. All the peoples of the earth are
nothing compared to him. He does as he
pleases among the angels of heaven and
among the people of the earth. No one
can stop him or say to him, 'What do you
mean by doing these things?'

"When my sanity returned to me, so did
my honor and glory and kingdom. My
advisers and nobles sought me out, and I
was restored as head of my kingdom, with
even greater honor than before.

"Now I, Nebuchadnezzar, praise and glorify
and honor the King of heaven. All his acts

are true, and he is able to humble the
proud." (Daniel 4:34–37)

As I read this, I saw once again what the ring of power can do to someone. If a person has been given a position of authority—no matter how capable, how clever, or how special they may be—when that ring goes on in the absence of humility, they will be just like Nebuchadnezzar or my friend's employee. The pride and arrogance hidden inside will be revealed to human society.

When you are given a ring of power to wear, things change. Without humility, you can become a human wrecking ball. That is not the way the Lord instructed us to live. He taught us that we are to be servants, not masters, and we are to consider ourselves the least and others greater. When I hire new staff members, I tell them that their new authority carries weight. What used to take a shout now only takes a whisper.

Since God chose you to be the holy people he loves, you must clothe yourselves
with tenderhearted mercy, kindness,
humility, gentleness, and patience.
(Colossians 3:12)

Wearing Our Ring

In some measure, we all wear the ring of power. How do we assure ourselves that we won't walk in the same way these men did when God gives us the opportunity to wear that ring? Scripture is full of answers to that question. In Luke 22:24–26, He gives us a glimpse:

The disciples bickered over which one of them would be considered the greatest in the kingdom. Jesus interrupted their argument, saying, "The kings and men of authority in this world rule oppressively over their subjects, claiming that they do it for the good of the people. They are obsessed with how others see them. But this is not your calling. You will lead by a different model. The greatest one among you will live as one called to serve others without honor. The greatest honor and authority is reserved for the one who has a servant heart." (TPT)

One of the most magnificent things that Jesus did demonstrates this answer best. It is told in the book of John, and occurs during Passover—right before Jesus was arrested. He was with the disciples and knew that this was the last supper, but the disciples didn't. These were the last hours on earth that He would have before He went to be with His Father.

I have been at the bedside of people who were living their last hours. When the family gathers for such a time, when they know their loved one is soon to be taken from them, people rethink their lives. Old grievances are forgotten. Suddenly, there is no room for petty things. The only things that matter are those things that are sacred. The time is revered. This is it. When those final hours arrive, all things change. Jesus knew He was in the final hours of His time with His disciples. What He did next would be the final lesson for them. What did He do? He taught them how to wear the ring:

> Now Jesus was fully aware that the Father had placed all things under his control, for he had come from God and was about to go back to be with him. So he got up from the meal and took off his outer robe, and took a towel and wrapped it around His waist. Then he poured water into a basin and began to wash the disciples' dirty feet and dry them with his towel.
>
> But when Jesus got to Simon Peter, he objected and said, "I can't let you wash my dirty feet—you're my Lord!"
>
> Jesus replied, "You don't understand yet the meaning of what I'm doing, but soon it will be clear to you."
>
> After washing their feet, he put his robe on and returned to his place at the table.
>
> "Do you understand what I just did?" Jesus said. "You've called me your teacher and lord, and you're right, for that's who I am. So if I'm your teacher and lord and have just washed your dirty feet, then you should follow the example that I've just set for you and wash one another's dirty feet. Now do for each other what I have just done for you. I speak to you timeless truth: a servant is not superior to

his master, and an apostle is never greater
that the one who sent him. So now, put
into practice what I have done for you,
and you will experience a life of happiness
enriched with untold blessings!" (John
13:3–7, 12–17 TPT)

If this lesson was so important that it was the very last thing
Jesus taught His disciples, then maybe we should give this lesson
first place in our hearts.

* * * * *

Think back. Have you experienced the effects of the ring of
power, either in your own life or in someone else's? As Christians,
we need to ask ourselves if there are places in our hearts where
we have misused the authority given to us.

**Father, help me to recognize where I have abused my
authority and have treated people with dishonor. I confess
this as sin and ask that you would forgive me. Please
continue to show me ways to honor and serve those who
you've placed in my life.**

Enter the Messengers

As you can see by now, one of the huge stumbling blocks in my life was that I simply judged the messengers that the Lord had sent to me and found them lacking. I disqualified them because, in my opinion, they didn't walk in the high standards that I thought were necessary to warrant my attention, much less my submission.

The Lord showed me another man who had encounters with "messengers." Jesus talked about him in Luke 4:27: "And many in Israel had leprosy in the time of the prophet Elisha, but the only one healed was Naaman, a Syrian."

Anytime Jesus points to someone in the Bible, we should take notice of that person because He is highlighting something about the person or their character that drew God to them. Here, Jesus is speaking about a character in the Old Testament who had something in his life that was significant enough to be given a place of notoriety in history. He was not a Jew but a Syrian. Therefore, "as the eyes of the Lord move to and fro throughout the earth that He may strongly support those whose heart is completely His" (2 Chronicles 16:9 NASB), what was it that the Lord found in this man—this Syrian, this foreigner—that He supported so well?

A Great Man

We find Naaman's story in 2 Kings 5, and right away it is established that he was a great man. He was a brave warrior, the commander of the entire army of Syria. He was actually second-in-command to the king of Syria. I think it would be safe for us to say he was probably similar to our vice president. Verse 1 says:

> Naaman, commander of the army of the
> king of Aram (Syria), was considered a
> great man by his king, and was highly
> respected because through Naaman the
> Lord had given victory to Aram (Syria). He
> was also a man of courage, but he was a
> leper. (2 Kings 5:1 AMP)

The story continues and tells how Naaman actually found out about Elisha:

> The Arameans (Syrians) had gone out in
> bands [as raiders] and had taken captive
> a little girl from the land of Israel; and she
> waited on Naaman's wife [as a servant].
> She said to her mistress, "I wish that my
> master [Naaman] were with the prophet

who is in Samaria! Then he would heal him
of his leprosy." (2 Kings 5:2–3 AMP)

This little girl, who was captured and taken as a slave, cared so much for her master that she desired him to be healed of his terrible affliction and told her masters about the prophet in her homeland who, she was convinced, could make this happen. After Naaman hears what this little slave girl has to say, he goes to the king and asks for permission to go to Israel so he can be healed. The king grants this honorable man permission to go.

> Then the king of Aram (Syria) said, "Go
> now, and I will send a letter to the king
> of Israel (Jehoram the son of Ahab)." So
> he left and took with him ten talents of
> silver and 6,000 shekels of gold, and ten
> changes of clothing.
> And he brought the letter to the king of
> Israel. It said, "And now when this letter
> comes to you, I will have sent my servant
> Naaman to you, so that you may heal him
> of his leprosy." When the king of Israel
> read the letter, he tore his clothes [in shock
> and outrage at the request] and said,
> "Am I God, to kill and to make alive, that
> this man sends to me [a request] to heal
> a man of his leprosy? Just consider [what
> he is asking] and see how he is seeking an
> opportunity [for a battle] with me."
> (2 Kings 5:5–7 AMP)

So now this has just become an international event. This greatly respected general, who is second-in-command to the king of Syria, is coming to Israel and causing an uproar. He has the attention of two kings and the heart of one. The other is terrified that the request cannot be accomplished and that it will be an excuse for war.

The Prophet

Enter Elisha. When Elisha hears of all this, he seems pretty chill.

> Now when Elisha the man of God heard
> that the king of Israel had torn his clothes,
> he sent word to the king, asking, "Why
> have you torn your clothes? Just let
> Naaman come to me, and he shall know
> that there is a [true] prophet in Israel."
> (2 Kings 5:8 AMP)

I want to set this up for you so you can see that Naaman was a man of great importance and highly esteemed in the land. He also was a man of great wealth. Watch as the story continues.

> So Naaman came with his horses and
> chariots and stopped at the entrance of
> Elisha's house. Elisha sent a messenger
> to him, saying, "Go and wash in the Jor-
> dan seven times, and your flesh will be
> restored to you and you will be clean."
> But Naaman was furious and went away

and said, "Indeed! I thought 'He would at
least come out to [see] me and stand and
call on the name of the Lord his God, and
wave his hand over the place [of leprosy]
and heal the leper.' Are not Abana and
Pharpar, the rivers of Damascus [in Aram],
better than all the waters of Israel? Could I
not wash in them and be clean?"
(2 Kings 5:9–12 AMP)

It is clear Naaman was a diplomat. And as a diplomat, he was accustomed to being received with honor and treated with respect. In his own country, when he arrived, it was expected that the people would come out to greet him. Anything less was unacceptable. So you can imagine how disrespected he felt when he arrived at Elisha's house with his entire entourage and was met a by a lowly servant.

If I could put this into a modern-day equivalent, it would be similar to a caravan of shiny black limos with their diplomatic flags, all waiting to be received by the man of God. If someone of importance, a highly esteemed government official like the vice president of the United States, were to show up at your house, could you imagine what it might look like? We would be seeing an impressive motorcade, police escort, black SUVs, military presence, secret service, etc. This was what happened when Naaman arrived at Elisha's house—and Elisha didn't even come out.

So Naaman was there, sitting on his chariot with his motorcade behind him and Elisha never came out to greet him. Understandably, Naaman got a bit ticked. Not only did Elisha refuse to see him, but he further offended this important man by sending out *his servant* to speak to him. Worse yet, the messenger came out to Naaman with a message from Elisha, saying, "Go wash yourself seven times in the Jordan river; then your skin will be restored and you will be healed."

Naaman was now furious. He was insulted. He had pictured what his healing would look like. He had created his story and had woven it all around his circumstances and assumed it would come to pass in just that way. *He would come to me,* he thought. This would have signified honor, recognition, and respect. He thought this man of God would understand his importance, his worth, his history, and his reputation, and then God would show His mighty power on Naaman's behalf. In his mind, Naaman thought, *I'm significant. That's why I will be healed.*

He thought Elisha would come and call on the name of the Lord his God and wave his hand over the leprosy and he would be healed. In Naaman's mind, he had created a story about his healing and imagined it would look a certain way. The actual events turned out to be much different from his expectations. Instead, he was asked to do something that was humiliating and beneath his station. Understandably, Naaman was furious. His encounter with this God was far different than he had imagined.

Naaman continued his rant: "Aren't the rivers where I live in Damascus better than any of the rivers here in Israel? Why should I need to wash in them to be healed?" And he turned and went away in a rage.

The Pivotal Point

Naaman was standing at a critical juncture in his life. At times it is difficult to understand God's purpose or trust His process. Many people have been so close to encountering God but have been offended—either God didn't meet them *when* they thought He was going to meet them or He didn't do things the *way* they thought He was going to do them. Sadly, these are often the people who are the most difficult to reach because they are the ones offended by God. Their experiences didn't match the stories that were woven around their expectations, and they harbor their resentments and often get stuck in them.

At this point, Naaman was offended and profoundly insulted. He was about to walk away. This decision would mean that he would go back home, still a leper. We need to understand what he was facing. Leprosy was a horrible plague. Its victims suffered tremendously. There was no cure. It was a demoralizing, degrading disease that was extremely contagious. Because the body of a leper was rotting, there was an appalling smell of death that radiated from them. They would ultimately become an outcast from society—and would die. So what was he thinking? Was he so proud and angry that he would not stoop to follow the prophet's instructions even if it cost him the healing that he desperately longed for?

> Then his servants approached him and said to him, "My father, if the prophet had told you to do some great thing, would you not have done it? How much more then, when he has said to you, 'Wash, and be clean?'" So he went down and plunged himself into the Jordan seven times, just as the man of God had said; and his flesh was restored like that of a little child and he was clean. (2 Kings 5:13–14 AMP)

The point that I want to highlight in the life of Naaman is that I believe that he actually *drew* God's healing presence to him. If you look at the course of events, he was dishonored by Elisha and offended by Elisha's servant. Even though he flew off the handle and walked away, we still see a glimmer of something very special about Naaman. He was teachable. There was something in his heart that allowed him to receive correction.

> Fools think their own way right, but the
> wise listen to others. (Proverbs 12:15)

Think about it. As a leader, this man was the second-most-important person in his nation. He was a fierce warrior, a greatly respected leader in the Syrian army, a highly decorated general who was enormously favored by his king. Imagine someone this important, with all the respect, leadership, and honor placed upon him, yet this man allowed God to do *what* He wanted to do in the *way* He wanted to do it. Because he was teachable and chose humility, Naaman was able to receive his healing.

However, I would like to point out that this goes deeper than Naaman just being teachable. The real catalyst in his healing was that he was able to receive correction and counsel from those "underneath" him. If you look at it, Naaman received instruction from a little foreign *servant* girl at the beginning of the story. Then, in the throes of the insults, when he was frustrated, angry, and ready to throw his hands up and just walk away, he listened to his *servants*.

I have found that the Lord often hides Himself in people who would ordinarily be difficult to receive from. I believe that the Lord hides "pieces" of Himself in everyone. In order for me to be blessed by that "piece" of the Lord that He has hidden in an individual, I have to learn from Naaman and humble myself in order to receive it. If I have any biases or any sort of criticism or prejudices, I have to rid myself of those in order to hear the nugget of truth that God has hidden inside the person standing before me.

"God resists you when you are proud but continually pours out grace when you are humble" (James 4:6 TPT). So what does humility look like? I might suggest that one of the characteristics of humility is being teachable. We have also just seen that being teachable is not just about receiving information—it's about *whom* you can receive information from.

Being teachable is the ability to bend. When our spouses, our children, or someone who doesn't seem like their life is together offers counsel or correction, we aren't truly teachable unless we're willing to listen. Naaman showed us his humility when he listened to those who clearly would have been seen as "lower" than him. I fully believe that is why Jesus spoke about him specifically to a crowd of people who hoped for healing. He was teaching them a major key to an encounter with God—humility.

* * * * *

Are you teachable? Think back and consider whether there have been people in your life who seemed insignificant or too small for you to receive instruction or correction from.

Father, give me the eyes to see those who you have placed in my life to give me wisdom and instruction.

18

Perils of Unbelief

I would like to share a revelation that I received from the book of Mark that impacted my life, but before I do, I need to back up a little and first share something the Lord gave me from the book of James: "But if any of you lacks wisdom, let him ask of God, who gives generously and without reproach" (James 1:5 NASB). As I saw this verse and read the words *without reproach*, I thought I would do a word study on *reproach* because it is a word that isn't often used in our daily vernacular. I found the synonyms insightful: without admonishing, without belittling, without chiding, without condemnation, without criticizing, without rebuking, without reprimand, without scolding, without shaming. I thought, *Oh my goodness! This is not how I thought God deals with His people.*

We all have our own mental picture of who God is. When we close our eyes and pray to Him, we all have a preconceived notion of what He's like. To some of us, God is really far away. Others pray and to them He is really close. Some people see Him as harsh, and some feel His gentleness. I always saw Him as loving—because we all know He loves us. Having said that, I also felt He was stern. I remember thinking, when I was a little boy, that God was mad most of the time. But now I am seeing something entirely different.

As I discovered this in James, I began to understand that He is telling me that I can go to Him and be assured that He will not reproach me. Wow! That was a brand-new paradigm for me. I began working through this new revelation that God had shown me about His character and His heart.

He showed me that He is the kind of God that I can go to and not be afraid that He will ever get tired of me asking over and over for His help—even when I mess up. He is gentle, He is tender, and He is patient with me and will always be there to help if I just ask Him. I felt such a deep, deep sense of peace and relief. This made such a powerful impact on me. I love the way The Passion Translation says it: "And if anyone longs to be wise, ask God for wisdom and He will give it! He won't see your lack of wisdom as an opportunity to *scold you over your failures* but He will overwhelm your failures with His generous grace."

I was so comforted by this verse that I ended up gravitating to it for months. I found myself meditating on it. It began to take root in my heart, but I still had to sort through stuff and not default to my old way of thinking, which was all about my own worthiness or my own sense of accomplishment. The more I interacted with the Lord, the more I realized that I finally had someone I could go to who would not tire of my needs or my failures—someone who would never do an eye roll or get fed up with me. I had never known such patience and kindness. I honestly can say that I had never known anyone in my life like that (though Becky comes the closest.)

A Question

Sometime later, I was reading in Mark 16:9. This Scripture takes place right after Jesus had been crucified and buried. Three days have passed. It was now the first day of the week, and Jesus appeared to Mary Magdalene. She was the first to see Him. She was so excited that she ran back to the disciples—who were hiding out, totally distraught, weeping and grieving—completely undone over all that had happened. Mary ran to them in all her exuberance and told them that Jesus had appeared to her—that she had seen Him! He was alive!

> Now Jesus, having risen [from death] early on the first day of the week, appeared first to Mary Magdalene, from whom He had driven out seven demons. She went and reported it to those who had been with Him, as they grieved and wept. And when they heard that He was alive and that she had seen Him, *they did not believe it.*
> (Mark 16:9–11 AMPC)

What? How could that possibly be? They didn't believe her? Then, as the next verse continues, Jesus then appeared in a different form to two of his disciples as they were walking down a road into the country. They ran back to the other disciples and told them the same thing—they saw Jesus ... alive! But look at what happened again:

> After this, He appeared in a different form
> to two of them as they were walking
> [along the way] into the country. And
> they returned [to Jerusalem] and told the
> others, but *they did not believe them either*.
> (Mark 16:12—13 AMPC)

What was going on? They didn't believe them either? Why? Why did they refuse to believe what their friends had just told them? It is especially hard to fathom because these people have been together, walking with Jesus for years. They knew these guys. They knew Mary Magdalene was tenaciously committed to the Lord. She was even at the cross with Him while all the rest but John ran and hid. Yet the disciples refused to believe all three of them. And the fact of the matter is that since there were three witnesses saying the same thing, their statements are actually confirmed true by law: "the facts of a case must be established by the testimony of two or three witnesses" (Deuteronomy 19:15). And Paul reiterates the same thing: "And I will make sure that by the testimony of two or three witnesses every matter will be confirmed" (2 Corinthians 13:1 TPT).

The hardest thing to grasp, though, is the fact that they had been there and had seen *with their own eyes* miracle after miracle that Jesus had performed. How many countless blind eyes were healed, how many countless lepers were healed, how many arms were extended, how many lame people walked? They were there when Jesus raised the little girl from the dead. They were also there when the Lord reached into the casket carrying the body of the only son of a poor widow in the village of Nain:

> When the Lord saw the grieving mother,
> his heart broke for her. With great tender-
> ness He said to her, "Please don't cry." Then
> He stepped up to the coffin and touched
> it. When the pallbearers came to a halt,
> Jesus said to the corpse, "Young man, I say
> to you, arise and live!" Immediately, the
> young man moved, sat up, and spoke to
> those nearby. Jesus presented the son to
> his mother, alive! (Luke 7:13–15 TPT)

They were witnesses and *participants* when over five thou-
sand were fed with a little boy's lunch.

> Then he had everyone sit down on the
> grass as he took the five loaves and two
> fish. He looked up to heaven, gave thanks
> to God, and broke the bread into pieces.
> He then gave it to his disciples, who in
> turn gave it to the crowds. And everyone
> ate until they were satisfied, for the food
> was multiplied in front of their eyes! They
> picked up the leftovers and filled up twelve
> baskets full! (Matthew 14:13–20 TPT)

They actually performed miracles themselves:

> Jesus gathered his twelve disciples and
> imparted to them his authority to cast out
> demons. Then he sent them out in pairs. . . .
> So they went out and preached publicly

that everyone should repent. They cast
out many demons and anointed many sick
people with oil and healed them.
(Mark 6:7, 12–13 TPT)

After this, the Lord Jesus formed thirty-five
teams among the other disciples. Each
team was two disciples, seventy in all,
and he commissioned them to go ahead
of him into every town he was about to
visit. … When the seventy missionaries
returned, they were ecstatic with joy, telling Him, "Lord, even the demons obeyed
us when we commanded them in your
name!" (Luke 10:1, 17–19 TPT)

They saw Jesus calm a storm so violent that experienced
fishermen were convinced that they were going to die. Jesus
walked on water in front of their very eyes—and Peter did too!
The disciples were also there in Bethany when Jesus was told that
Lazarus was beginning to stink after having been dead for four
days. Then they watched as Jesus called him forth and Lazarus
walked out of his tomb! I could go on and on and on recounting
all that the disciples saw, but I think John sums it up and emphasizes the point I'm trying to make: "Jesus did countless things that
I haven't included here. And if every one of his works were written
one by one, I suppose that the world itself wouldn't have enough
room to contain the books that would have to be written!" (John
21:25 TPT).

The Reproach

Having said all that, watch what happened next:

> Afterward He appeared to the Eleven
> [apostles themselves] as they reclined
> at table: and *He reproved and reproached*
> *them for their unbelief* (their lack of faith)
> and *their hardness of heart*, because they
> had refused to believe those who had
> seen Him and looked at Him attentively
> after He had risen [from death].
> (Mark 16:14 AMPC)

Jesus *reproached* them? But I thought that it says in James that Jesus *doesn't* reproach? Yet here, He is absolutely reproaching them. So what is being said? By taking a closer look at James, we see that the Lord is telling us that if we come to Him *needy,* He will never reproach us. We can come to Him, saying, "I need wisdom, and there is no way for me to get wisdom on my own. Lord, I recognize that I have no ability to grasp wisdom unless you, the Source of wisdom, divinely impart it to me. I know there is no way, apart from you, that I will get it."

Then, it's like the Lord says, "I love that heart! The fact that you recognize that. I will absolutely give that to you, and I will never scold you for asking me. I will never reproach you for coming to me. I understand that you might feel like you are totally over your head. And that's okay. That's the way I designed this world—that's the way I designed your world. You will constantly be in over your head, but the fact that you are coming to me for my help … I love it!"

That is a completely different scenario than what we are seeing here with the disciples, who had been with Jesus, who had witnessed all the amazing things that I just talked about, and yet they *refused to believe*. Therefore, what I think is being said here is that *believing is a choice*. Jesus was reproaching them for their *choice*. They had a choice to believe the messengers He had specifically sent to them, but they refused to believe them. I suspect He may have called them into account more sternly because of all they had witnessed.

It was as though He was asking them, "How can you refuse to believe when your eyes have seen countless miracles that happened daily with me? Do you not remember all that was done by my Father through me? We talked about that. If watching the blind see, the lame walk, the lepers healed, and the dead return to life wasn't impressive enough for you to remember, could you not remember the time I subdued nature by walking out to you on the water? Or how could you forget the time we were at sea and you thought death was certain in that ferocious storm, but then you watched as the forces of nature bowed at my word and those turbulent seas turn to glass?

"You have been privileged to witness more than any other living beings on earth. Why did you not believe me when I said I would return to you? Why did you choose to refuse to believe the messengers I sent to you—those whom I chose from among you, those whom you know, those who are your friends, who walked together with us for years—to tell you that I was no longer dead? Why did you not believe them? How could you choose to not believe that I could be raised from the dead after I told you that I would be? What cause did I ever give you to not believe me?"

When the full impact of what was happening here hit me,

it was like a blow to my spirit. The Lord was saying was that belief or unbelief is a *decision*. It is a *choice*. We decide. He would have never reproached them otherwise. So it boils down to this: Are we going to trust Him and take Him at His word and *choose* to believe the things He says, *choose* to remember the things He has done, *choose* to remember that He is faithful? Or are we going to lean toward our own understanding and *choose* not to believe because it could be too good to be true? Or *choose* not to believe it could happen because He would never do something like that for me? Or *choose* not to believe because I can't afford to get my hopes up? Or *choose* not to believe because it is just too risky— it is just too much to have my heart sick again? Would I rather *choose* to self-protect and prepare for disappointment than risk hoping?

The other thing that Jesus called them out on was their "hardness of heart." Once again, how could this happen? How could the disciples of Jesus—the ones who were chosen by Him, loved by Him, called by Him, who spent more time with Him than anyone on earth, the ones who were personally coached by Him and saw mind-bending miracles take place—possibly have *hardened their hearts*?

I desperately wanted to find answers to this, and I had to start by finding out what *hardness of heart* actually means. Psalm 95 says that the Israelites hardened their hearts at Meribah: "The Lord says, 'Don't harden your hearts as Israel did at Meribah, as they did at Massah. For there your ancestors tested and tried my patience, even though they saw everything I did'" (Psalms 95:8).

As I was studying this, I came to this conclusion: A hardness of heart is the refusal to believe that God will be as faithful to me today as He has been in the past.

* * * * *

Father, forgive me for forgetting the good things that you have done for me in my life and for disregarding your faithfulness. I confess my doubt and fear as sin. I choose to focus on your Word, which says that you will continue to be faithful to me today as you have been for me in the past.

The Place of Testing

There is another place in Scripture where the Lord exposed hearts that are hardened.

> At the Lord's command, the whole community of Israel left the wilderness of Sin and moved from place to place. Eventually they camped at Rephidim, but there was no water for the people to drink. So once more the people complained against Moses. "Give us water to drink!" they demanded.
>
> "Quiet!" Moses replied. "Why are you complaining against me? And why are you testing the Lord?"
>
> But tormented by thirst, they continued to argue with Moses. "Why did you bring us

out of Egypt? Are you trying to kill us, our children, and our livestock with thirst?" Then Moses cried out to the Lord, "What should I do with these people? They are ready to stone me!" The Lord said to Moses, "Walk out in front of the people. Take your staff, the one you used when you struck the water of the Nile, and call some of the elders of Israel to join you. I will stand before you on the rock at Mount Sinai. Strike the rock, and water will come gushing out. Then, the people will be able to drink." So Moses struck the rock as he was told, and water gushed out as the elders looked on. Moses named the place Massah (which means "test") and Meribah (which means "arguing") because the people of Israel argued with Moses and tested the Lord by saying, "Is the Lord here with us or not?" (Exodus 17:1–7)

We see that the children of Israel were being led by the Lord in the wilderness after they had been freed from the slavery and oppression of Egypt. As we know, Moses was their leader. They got to a place to camp called Rephidim and they were thirsty. They discovered there was no water. The people lost it on Moses: "What are you thinking, Moses? Can't you see there is no water in this place? Why did you even bring us out of Egypt?" It's like they were saying, "Slavery wasn't all that bad. At least we had water! What are you trying to do, kill us?"

Moses was undone. He was getting tired of these people and their persistent bickering and complaining. I can only imagine what Moses is thinking: *Why are you taking this out on me? Just be quiet! I'm only going by what God told me to do. I didn't bring you here. I promise, God Himself did! And I knew nothing about the water situation!*

Then Moses went before the Lord and poured out his heart to Him: "Lord, these people are losing it here. They are about to kill me! They are gathering stones as we speak. What am I to do?"

The Lord gave Moses specific instructions: "This is what I want you to do. I want you to go grab your staff (make sure it's the one you used on the Nile), bring the elders, and meet me at the rock. I will stand before you on it. Then I want you to strike that rock, water will come pouring out, and the people can have their drink."

Let's look closer at what the Lord was saying. He said to grab two things: the staff and the elders. If we go back to the beginning of the book of Exodus, all the way back to the time when Moses had just been called by the Lord to deliver the Israelites, we see some interesting things.

The Israelites didn't understand what was happening at this point, but the Lord had just declared that the time has finally come to deliver His people out of their bondage. God told Moses to tell the elders what He had instructed him to do. But Moses had little confidence in himself and asked the Lord what he was to do if the elders didn't believe him. He asked Him, "How will I be able to prove to them that you're with me?"

"What is that in your hand, Moses?" the Lord asked.

"Well, Lord, it's my shepherd's staff."

"Throw it down."

"Uh … okay." The staff turned into a snake.

"Now pick it up." It turned back into a staff.

Moses then gathered the elders and told them what had happened. He threw down the staff and they saw the serpent for themselves. Then they went before Pharaoh. The elders watched as the staff was thrown down and all saw it turn into a snake. They watched as the Egyptian sorcerers' matched that feat and their staffs also turned into snakes. Everyone was shocked as the staff of Moses ate the snakes of the sorcerers.

Man, oh, man—if only this staff could talk! Wouldn't it be amazing to hear all the stuff that it had seen? "Well, after I ate the Egyptians' staffs, Moses took me out and I was raised over the Nile and it turned to blood. That was a mess. Then he took me out and lifted me over the waters there in Egypt, and frogs crawled out from everywhere. Not long after that, Moses told Aaron to raise me up and strike the ground. Billions of gnats appeared all over everything and everyone. This kind of stuff went on for a while. There were flies, locusts, and at one point, all of the Egyptians' livestock got sick and died. Every time I was raised up, something big happened. People got boils, the sun stopped shining—but it didn't stop until that horrible night when their firstborn children died. That's when they took me to the Red Sea."

This staff was a vital, integral part of all the amazing miracles that took place. It was present at every incredible event—and it was one of the things the Lord told Moses to bring with him to the rock. I believe He told Moses to bring it because it was a symbol to the people of all the miracles God had performed for them in the past.

And the elders? Well, they saw all these things happen— they were witnesses to it all. At the very beginning, the elders were there. They were there right when all of these miraculous, monumental events started. Before Moses ever approached Pharaoh, they saw the staff turn into a snake. They also watched Moses put his hand in his cloak and pull it out leprous. Then they witnessed him bring it back out perfectly healthy again (Exodus 4:1–8, 30–31). They were there at the beginning when this wild adventure began. Therefore, it's my belief that the Lord told Moses to gather the elders because the elders represent the ones who were with him in the beginning, the ones who had history with the Lord, who were eyewitnesses to God's miraculous power.

Now, going back to the angry, thirsty Israelites …

The Lord was telling Moses to gather the elders, *the ones who have history with the Lord*, and make sure to bring the staff, *the symbol of God's power*, and *I will meet you on the rock*. Then I want you to strike that rock and water will pour forth.

Things happened just as the Lord told Moses they would: "So Moses struck the rock as he was told, and water gushed out as the elders looked on" (Exodus 17:6).

If we fast-forward several decades, the Israelites again found themselves in a very similar situation. The Lord brought them to another place with no water and, just like before, they freaked out. You would think that someone somewhere would have said, "Wait, I remember this happening before! God sure did take care of us back then. I remember watching that water gushing like crazy, coming right out of that rock!" Unfortunately, not much had changed:

> There was no water for the people to drink
> at that place, so they rebelled against
> Moses and Aaron. The people blamed

Moses and said, "If only we had died in the Lord's presence with our brothers! Why have you brought the congregation of the Lord's people into the wilderness to die, along with our livestock? Why did you make us leave Egypt and bring us here to this terrible place? This land has no grain, no figs, no grapes, no pomegranates, and no water to drink!"

Moses and Aaron turned away from the people and went to the entrance of the Tabernacle where they fell face down on the ground. The glorious presence of the Lord appeared to them, and the Lord said to Moses, "You and Aaron must take the staff and assemble the entire community. As the people watch, speak to the rock over there, and it will pour out its water. You will provide enough water from the rock to satisfy the whole community and their livestock."

So Moses did what he was told. He took the staff from the place where it was kept before the Lord. Then he and Aaron summoned the people to come and gather at the rock. "Listen, you rebels!" he shouted. "Must we bring you water out of this rock?" Then Moses raised his hand and struck the rock twice with the staff, and

water gushed out. So the entire commu-
nity and their livestock drank their fill.
But the Lord said to Moses and Aaron,
"Because you did not trust me enough to
demonstrate my holiness to the people of
Israel, you will not lead them into the land
I am giving them!" This place was known
as the waters of Meribah (which means
"arguing") because there the people of
Israel argued with the Lord, and there he
demonstrated his holiness among them.
(Numbers 20:2–13)

The Lord was trying to tell Moses that this time, take what you've seen and bring it forward in your heart and speak to the rock. But, sadly, Moses didn't honor what the Lord told him to do and, in his anger, struck the rock. Water still gushed out of the rock, but Moses would find out that there were grave consequences to his actions. The Lord told him, "Because you didn't treat me as holy, you're not going to go forward. You will not be able to lead my people into the promised land."

The Lord was telling Moses that he was treating Him like everybody else: "Moses, you're treating me like someone who doesn't have the power to deliver—and I am holy! You're treating me as a person who won't follow through on what they say! I am in a class all by myself—uncreated. I am the One who has no terminology that will describe me. I am completely Other Than—I am holy. Because you have not treated me as holy, and because you did not take the opportunity I gave you to show my people my holiness, you will not be able to lead them into the promised land."

Paul gives insight to this story and draws out an interesting parallel:

> My dear fellow believers, you need to understand that all of our Jewish ancestors who walked through a wilderness long ago were under the glory cloud and passed through the waters of the sea on both sides. They were all baptized into the cloud of glory, not the fellowship of Moses, and into the sea. They all ate the same heavenly manna and drank water from the same *spiritual rock that traveled with them—and that Rock was Christ Himself.* (1 Corinthians 10:1–4 TPT)

Refreshing in the Hard Place

How, then, do we get water from a rock and how do we keep our hearts from becoming hardened? Water, metaphorically, represents refreshing. Therefore, how do we get refreshing from a hard place? Looking again at the story, remember that God led them to this hard place, a place of impossibility. He met them there and miraculously brought the water of refreshing to them. To get water from a rock—to get refreshing—we do what God told Moses to do. Use *the staff*—the reminder of God's power—remembering all the places in the past where the Lord has come through for you. Then bring in the *elders,* the ones who have history with us and with the Lord who are witnesses to His faithfulness. These are the ones who can remind us that He can do it again. Then you *speak* to the Rock, and say, "I remember when you did this … and I know you will do it again." So what He is saying is this: "Take all you've seen and bring it forward in your heart, speak to the Rock, and expect refreshing."

* * * * *

"The Lord says, 'Don't harden your hearts as Israel did at Meribah, as they did at Massah. For there your ancestors tested and tried my patience, even though they saw everything I did'" (Psalms 95:8).

What are the good things you have seen the Lord do for you in your life?

God emphasizes the necessity of remembering all the good things that He has done for us. It is imperative for us to remember these things to keep our hearts from being hardened. When you find yourself in a hard place, it is often difficult to remember all of the good things that the Lord has done for you in the past without recording them in some way. So if you haven't done so before, I would highly recommend that you begin now.

20

Be Careful How You Listen

"So pay attention to *how* you hear.
To those who listen to my teaching,
more understanding will be given.
But for those who are not listening,
even what they think they understand
will be taken away from them."

Luke 8:18

Then he added, "Pay close attention to *what* you hear.
The closer you listen, the more understanding you
will be given—and you will receive even more."

Mark 4:24

Be careful *what* you listen to, be careful *how* you hear … This is an important warning to us. When I saw this, I noticed this was what the children of Israel and the disciples were doing—but so was I. *How* was I hearing? Well, I was hearing through a filter that judged the messengers as defective. They were disqualified in my way of thinking, so that's what I was hearing. To me, they had flaws that neutralized them from being able to carry the message that God gave them for me and for my benefit. But I could not hear it—just like the disciples and the children of Israel.

Be careful *how* you hear, and be careful *what* you hear, because if we don't mix faith with our hearing, all that's being said will fall null and void and not profit us.

Regarding *what* you hear, look at what Jesus said once more: "Pay close attention to *what* you hear. The closer you listen, the more understanding you will be given—and you will receive even more."

Have you noticed that things like unbelief, complaining, murmuring, and gossip seem to be contagious? Each one of these affects our ability to hear truth. When we listen to careless words, words of fear, and unbelieving words, we put ourselves at risk of being unable to hear truth. We need to make sure *what* we are hearing is God's truth, so that the closer we listen, the more understanding we will receive—and even be given more. And if we don't, we risk hardening our hearts.

> But when they saw him walking on the
> water, they cried out in terror, thinking it
> was a ghost. There were terrified when
> they saw him. But Jesus spoke to them
> at once, "Do not be afraid," he said. "Take
> courage! I am here!" Then he climbed into

the boat, and the wind stopped. They were totally amazed, *for they still didn't understand the significance of the miracle of the loaves. Their hearts were too hard to take it in.* (Mark 6:49–52)

How do we harden our hearts? As I mentioned before, by refusing to believe Him even though we have seen His faithfulness before. When we choose to believe that He will not be faithful in our present-day circumstance, even though He has proven Himself faithful in the past, that choice is what causes our hearts to become hardened.

What to Hold on To

I once heard a college professor lecture at a Christian university. He began by asking his class one simple question: "Why did Jesus come into the world?" He opened up the question for discussion, and in this class of twenty or thirty students, only a handful attempted to answer him. I suspected he sensed their apprehension because he clarified, "My objective is not to embarrass anybody, but to get us to think."

Then, one by one, the students took stabs at answering the question. "Jesus came into the world to save us," one student said.

The professor answered, "You're right, but in this case, that's not the answer that I'm looking for."

"To deliver us from the power of the devil," another student answered.

Again, the professor replied, "You're right, but that's not the answer I'm looking for either."

"To redeem us from a life of sin," another tried.

"Yes, and actually, no. Still not the answer I'm looking for."

More students made attempts such as "To bring healing," "To do the Father's will," and "To reveal the Father," but none of those were what the professor was looking for. After more failed attempts, he asked again, "Why was Jesus born? For what reason was He brought into this world, and what purpose was He to accomplish?"

He told the students that Jesus answered each of these questions in Scripture. He gave them a hint from John 18: "For this reason I was born and for this reason I came into the world, to _____."

Let me break from my story here and paraphrase the scene in the Bible prior to the professor's verse. Jesus had already been arrested by the Jewish leaders and they had just handed him over to Pilate, the Roman governor:

> Pilate ... summoned Jesus and asked him,
> "Are you the king of the Jews?"
> "Is that your own idea," Jesus asked, "or did
> others talk to you about me?"
> "Am I a Jew?" Pilate replied. "Your own
> people and chief priests handed you over
> to me. What is it you have done?"
> Jesus said, "My kingdom is not of this
> world. If it were, my servants would fight
> to prevent my arrest by the Jewish leaders.
> But my kingdom is from another place."
> "You are a king, then!" said Pilate.
> Jesus answered, "You say that I am a king.
> In fact, the reason I was born and came

into the world is *to testify to the truth.*
Everyone on the side of truth listens to
me." (John 17:33–37 NIV)

The professor's question was finally answered. The reason Jesus was born and came into this world was to testify to the *truth.*

You could see the shock on the students' faces and on mine. There was the answer, right before our eyes. Jesus clearly said that the reason He came into the world was to *testify to the truth.*

But "'What is Truth?' retorted Pilate" (John 17:38 NIV).

The Answer

What an astoundingly important question! This is undeniably *the most* important question of the ages. What is truth? How do *you* define truth? What is truth to you? Most of us would answer that question in some form or fashion that would make it subjective. In other words, most people would say, "It is what I believe truth is," or "It is what I perceive truth is," or, "It is what the general consensus of people would say it is." But look at what else Jesus said: "Everyone on the side of truth listens to me" (John 18:37 NIV).

What was He saying? Jesus said that everyone on the *side* of truth listens to Him. That tells me there is another *side* that is not truth, where people *don't* listen. Jesus told us to be careful *how* we listen. A person can hear someone speak and recite word for word what was said but still not be *listening.*

If we go back to the question "What is truth?" we need to find the answer and make sure we are on the right side—the side of truth. How would we answer if we were asked? As I said, most people tend to define it as subjective: truth is what *seems* right. But there has to be something greater than ourselves that defines truth.

In John 17, Jesus knew He was about to be arrested and the remainder of His time on earth was short. He was wrapping things up before He went to His death. Here, He was commending His disciples to His Father:

> "I am coming to you now, but I say these things while I am still in the world, so that they may have the full measure of my joy within them. I have given them your word and the world has hated them, for they are not of the world any more that I am of the world. My prayer is not that you take them out of the world but that you protect them from the evil one." (John 17:13–15 NIV)

We see that in these last hours, Jesus was asking His Father to take care of His loved ones that had been given to Him. During these last precious moments, He asked one more thing. What was the final request Jesus made of His Father before He left this earth? "Sanctify them by the truth" (John 17:17 NIV).

Sanctify is another word that is seldom used in today's vernacular, but it means to "set apart." Jesus was asking His Father to set His disciples apart in truth. Set them apart in *truth*? Why didn't He ask to set them apart in power? Set them apart in love? Why truth?

When we think about truth in a person's life, we could say truth is like a compass. We usually live our lives according to what we believe truth is. It is what we perceive our "true north" will be.

Jesus was in essence saying, "Father, these dear ones that you have given me are going to need guidance. For them to continue on this course, they are going to need direction—they are going to need a compass for their lives." He knew that there were so many distractions, so many falsehoods, as well as doctrines of demons and even doctrines of their own flesh, but He knew that the *truth* would keep them grounded and rooted and firmly on the right path. He knew the degree of their effectiveness would be determined by how much truth they would walk in.

"Sanctify them in truth." So, once again, what is truth?

"Your word is truth" (John 17:17 NIV). Truth is the Word of God. We now have the revelation of what truth really is. This provides our compasses with a true north. However, it also enables us to see what is on the other side—what truth is not. It is not error, it is not self-contradictory, and it is not deception. It is also not relativism, which means that all points of view are equally valid and all truth is related to each individual. Relativism means that all moral positions, all religious systems, all art forms, all political movements, are truths that are relative to the individual. This suggests that all truth is subjective. In other words, "If it seems good to me, then it must be true." However, "There is a way which seems right to a man, but its end is the way of death" (Proverbs 16:25 NASB). So the danger in having subjective meanings of truth is that, ultimately, it produces death.

Truth is often defined as that which is considered to be the supreme reality and to have the ultimate meaning and value of existence. Jesus was speaking from an eternal perspective: "Sanctify them in your truth. Your Word is truth." His eternal perspective, or His supernatural perspective, or His supreme perspective supersedes our natural one. When He said, "Your Word is truth," He was saying, "Father, your Word is the supreme reality and defines the ultimate meaning and value of existence."

God's Word is truth. It is our guide, our compass. We must stay in the truth of God's Word. We must find out what His Word says about our circumstances, about our health, about our finances, about our perspectives, and about all aspects of our lives.

Though this book is all about letting go of the need to be right, I wanted to make sure we remember that there are things we never let go of. I wanted to make sure that I'm clearly saying that letting go of the need to be right in no way means that we should ever let go of the truth—ever. His Word should always be true north in the compass of our life.

What I am suggesting is that we consider letting go of our need to defend ourselves and insist on our rightness in order to protect our reputations, specifically within the context of relating to the people around us—spouses, children, friends, coworkers, pastors, and bosses. Our reputations, opinions, and positions of authority are never issues of truth that need defending, but merely opportunities and callings to serve.

I want to point all of us toward a posture of humility where we pause to consider the perspective of others. When a person has an opinion different from our own, maybe they have a point that we should consider. This is not weakness; this is wisdom that will release the power of humility upon your life.

The way of a fool is right in his own eyes,
but a wise man is he who listens to counsel.
(Proverbs 12:15 NASB).

I hope this book will inspire us to take an honest, inward look at ourselves and ask the question, "How would I know if I was wrong?" Remind yourself, "Maybe ... the person who needs to change the most is me. Maybe ... some of the issues I am facing are not actually with the people around me. Maybe ... God is using those people to speak to me about areas in my life that I cannot see."

Whether you are a pastor, student, business leader, entrepreneur, husband, wife, parent, or child, I encourage you to consider the possibility that God may be using the people He put in your life—the very people with whom you are the closest—as vessels for His voice. They are placed there to help us correct our hearts so that we are free to move forward in the power of humility.

May His favor be upon us as we walk toward the destinies and callings He has on our lives.

* * * * *

The Lord spoke to Moses. He said, "Tell Aaron and his sons, 'Here is how I want you to bless the Israelites. Say to them,
"'May the Lord bless you and take good care of you. May the Lord smile on you and be gracious to you. May the Lord look on you with favor and give you peace.'
"In that way they will put the blessing of my name on the Israelites. And I will bless them."
(Numbers 6:22–27 NIrV)

A Testimony of Letting Go

So what might it look like when we are actually willing to let go of the need to be right? Or, worded another way, what would it look like if we were willing to be wrong? Or maybe even willing to just consider the fact that we might be wrong? What would it look like in our relationships if we didn't have to be right?

A dear friend of mine, a well-respected person in our community, shared a story of how this impacted her life. I had shared my experience with her and it moved her deeply. Sometime later, she told me of an incident when she went out on a limb and applied this revelation in a most unusual setting.

At the time, my friend was managing a medical facility in which many physicians practiced. A situation came up that had caused a division among the doctors. A meeting was called and a "meeting of the minds" was needed, but it looked hopeless. Everyone was dug in. As each doctor came in, they sat on the side with those who shared the same opinions regarding the situation to be discussed, so the room was clearly divided. It was a face-off. The tension in the room was tangible. Few spoke. Everyone was sitting in the awkward silence ready for a war.

My friend was to preside over the meeting. Even though she was a bit hesitant, she had determined what she was going to do. Looking directly at each one of them, she opened the meeting with these words, "Okay, so what would it look like if you were wrong?"

She said they were shocked at first. What an unusual opening. But something unforeseen then happened. Each of them, one by one, sat back in their chairs and didn't say a word. Before, they were postured for a fight. But as each one pondered the question, the atmosphere changed in the room. From that point, it didn't take long at all to settle the dispute, and everyone went on their way happy as could be. She told me what she had witnessed was remarkable, as doctors have a harder time not being right because that usually means a patient will suffer because of it. But when this group paused and considered it, humility brought the solution and peace. She said it was an astounding thing to witness.

If this has that kind of impact on a room full of professionals—colleagues from varied backgrounds—what kind of impact could it have on our personal relationships? What if we asked ourselves if we could let Jesus love us enough that we could be wrong and that would be okay? Or if we could love others enough to let them be right?

If we truly grasped the depths of the love that God has for us, I believe that our identities would be satisfied with our worth in Him and we wouldn't be affected by man's opinions. When we judge ourselves against other people, it is simply a counterfeit. The opinion of man then becomes an idol, and I believe our

Father loves us so much that He will not let a counterfeit become our identity. He loves for us to have success and He loves us in the midst of our failures, but our identity cannot be in our successes or our failures. Those cannot be our value system. Our value system is what we measure ourselves against, and He alone must be our value system.

As in my life, He loved me so much that He allowed me to experience all the hurt and frustration and unpleasant circumstances that caused me to get stuck enough to get desperate enough to be able to finally hear Him. He wanted me to be free of the counterfeit identity that plagued my life and restricted me from the intimacy with the Father that I was yearning for.

You've heard people say to not despise the process? I would heartily agree. I know from experience that the process of life can be painful and messy and uncomfortable, but He is found in the process. That's where He meets us.

"The Lord is close to the brokenhearted; he rescues those whose spirits are crushed." (Psalm 34:18). That is exactly what He did for me, and He will do it for you too.

About the Author

Jeff Dollar is a local pastor and international speaker. Jeff and his wife, Becky, have been senior pastors at Grace Center in Franklin, Tennessee, since 2007. They have pioneered a move of unity and relationship among leaders, resulting in local and international ministry partnerships; a training school that equips students and sends them around the world; and the adoption of a village in Mozambique, in support of Heidi Baker and Iris Ministries. Jeff also ministers globally, bringing an impartation of Grace Center's value for hosting the presence of God. Jeff longs to see hearts restored and loves to teach on the subject of practical wisdom.